Attitudes in Design Education

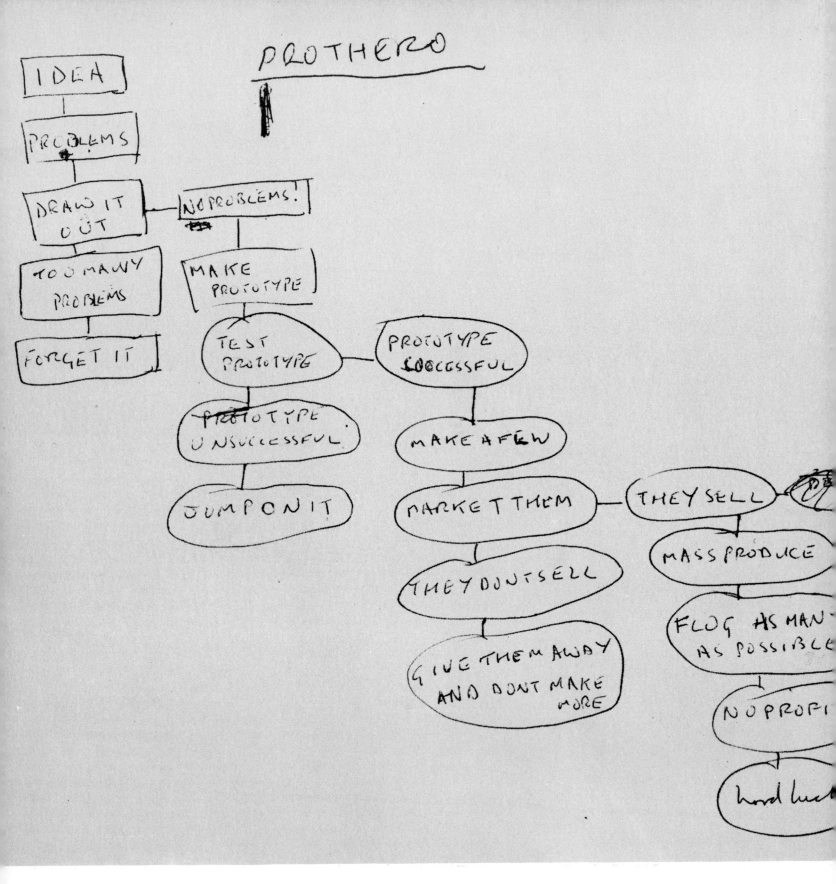

Diagram of the design process by
a London schoolboy.

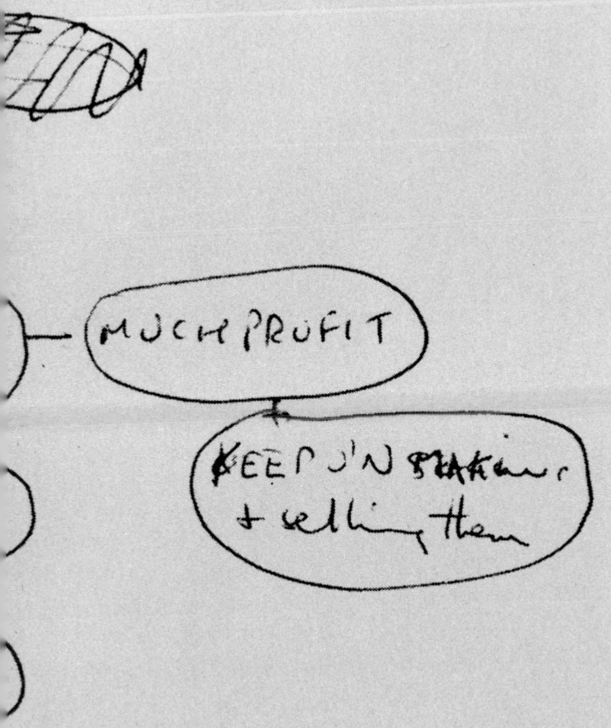

Attitudes in Design Education

Edited by Ken Baynes

Contents		page

Lund Humphries | London

Acknowledgements

Individuals, schools, colleges and other organizations have all contributed to this book. As editor I am, of course, particularly grateful to the authors, but behind them stand many others who have made the work possible. Peter Green, Head of the Teacher Training Department at Hornsey College of Art, deserves special thanks – without him, and the staff and students at the college, I would not have become so involved in this very important area of design education. Special thanks should go too to all the schools who have so readily supplied information and photographs, help, and often enough, hospitality.

Many of the photographs in the book have been specially taken by Christopher Ridley –without his sympathetic approach to the subject of young people at work much would be missing that is important.

My wife, Kate, has played a vital part in the editing and production of the book and is, as usual, really entitled to be called joint-editor. In my office Mrs Ann Roberts, Mrs Anne Porter and Mrs Mona Adams have all contributed in terms of research, typing and proof-reading. The book is in the true sense a co-operative project – the outcome of enthusiasm and hard work by many busy people. My dedication is to the busiest of them all – to the teachers in the schools.
Ken Baynes Battersea March 1969

Acknowledgements to Photographers

1–6 Christopher Ridley; 7 Pace; 8 The Times; 10 G H Metters; 12–14 Christopher Ridley; 15 Dennis Chapman; 17 and 18 Dennis Chapman; 19–22 Julian Sheppard; 30–35 Christopher Ridley; 36 Hornsey College of Art; 37 Christopher Ridley; 38 Hornsey College of Art; 42 and 43 Christopher Ridley; 45 and 46 Christopher Ridley; 50–52 Hornsey College of Art; 55–59 Christopher Ridley; 61 Hornsey College of Art; 62–71 Christopher Ridley; 72 and 73 Hornsey College of Art; 76 Hornsey College of Art; 77–83 Christopher Ridley; 84–87 Hornsey College of Art; 90–92 Christopher Ridley; 97 Hornsey College of Art; 102–106 Christopher Ridley; 115–117 Christopher Ridley; 127–130 Christopher Ridley; 153–157 John Hunnex; 187–189 Keystone Press Agency Ltd; 203–212 John Hunnex; 220 Christopher Ridley; 223 Westchester Rockland Newspaper Group; 226–234 Council of Industrial Design; 240–242 Council of Industrial Design.

Design Education in Schools

1 INTRODUCTION

KEN BAYNES A.R.C.A., A.S.I.A.

In my previous book *Industrial Design and the Community* I wrote:

'As things stand our (design) education system is doing only half its job. It succeeds – more or less – in training professional designers by giving them a relatively long period of intense specialization in a small number of schools and colleges. What happens is open to criticism in some respects, but at least the basis for growth and development is there, and professional design education in Britain looks healthier today than it has ever done before. In the same way there is a coherent system for producing architects and engineers. What emphatically does not happen is the complementary general education which would give these future professionals a better starting point and, at the same time, give the community at large some sort of basis on which to cope with the intensely difficult design problems of the modern urban environment and modern technology.'

At that time (February 1967), I would certainly have doubted the possibility of a book like this one appearing only about two years later. Although I was already in touch with many hopeful developments, and had seen for myself something of the conditions and related potential that existed in the secondary school system, the speed with which developments have taken place seems astonishing. It is as though this whole problem, its importance and therefore the determination to solve it, has quite suddenly come into focus. In fact, a more careful analysis in 1967 might have shown what would happen, for it is true that many of the events which have recently taken place are the result of planning, preparation and hard work over long periods.

There is something quite strange here. As John Kingsland shows in his contribution, the need for practical, technologically biased secondary education was clearly recognized by the end of the nineteenth century while, at the same time, the state of the industrial urban environment was a matter of constant concern to moral and aesthetic philosophers. Yet the type of school which would begin to solve the problem, and which did eventually lead to the kind of work described by Mr Kingsland, persistently continued to have a low status in relation to the educational structure as a whole. In its turn, art education gradually turned away from environmental problems to concentrate on the development of individual expressiveness; between the two world wars this was a breath of fresh air, but the attitude turned its back on industry and technology. Even the early educational work of the Council of Industrial Design tended to be cut down through lack of funds. The picture is of a continuing concern constantly frustrated. Suddenly the same arguments find a sympathetic audience, and there seems a real chance that changes of lasting benefit will be achieved.

There are probably two main reasons why these events are taking place in Britain at this particular moment. One is the complex change which is associated with the final destruction of aristocratic society and the dismantling of world responsibilities. It involves coming to terms with certain facts – that most people live in suburbia or in large industrial cities, that patronage is dispersed throughout the mass market, that traditional social and moral codes are increasingly unworkable in contemporary conditions. An aspect of this is a tremendous desire to understand the mechanisms and possibilities of mass industrial culture. Young people are less and less seduced by a vision of a lost rural or imperial past, more and more concerned to build out of the resources of the present. In a real sense the situation is new, born only with the coming of mass literacy, radio, television, the cinema, holidays abroad,

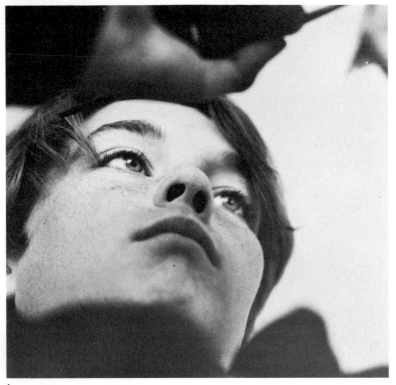

1

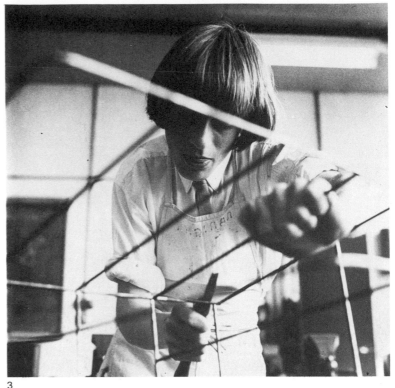

3

2

1 The kind of activity described in this book is built on a long tradition of practical work in schools. For many years art, woodwork and metalwork and housecraft have played an important role, and one which many children have found of absorbing interest. Now these areas are being drawn closer together by a common desire to relate their studies more directly to the kind of urban, industrial society that we live in. It is in this context that design education is becoming so important.

2 Children from a school in Leicestershire with objects they have made in the art room.

3 Woodwork and metalwork have often suffered from a lack of educational status in the past, but they offer a whole range of experiences which children find fascinating and rewarding.

4

6

4 and 5 A big variety of practical activities already exist in many schools – shown here is sculpture in Leicestershire, printing at Uppingham College.
6 Housecraft attracts children because of its obvious relevance to adult life – it also brings them into direct contact with many domestic products under conditions which allow them to be critically compared.

5

and widening horizons of every kind. The interest in the practical possibilities offered by design education is based on its obvious relevance to the kind of society which is emerging.

The second reason, intimately related to the first, is the climate which now exists for change in education. As Anthony Horrocks argues, one of the main driving forces behind the feeling for reform is dissatisfaction with past performance. Both art and handicraft teaching have often had only a marginal effect, frequently concentrating on those children with special aptitude. It has been very rare for either subject to achieve a central place in the life of a school. The healthy thing is that the specialist teacher's response is ceasing to be one of blaming the ignorance of the public or the crassness of authority; the growing determination is to solve the problem by making the work done relevant to the needs of young people growing up in a mass industrial, largely urban, society.

In this context, it is worth saying a little more about the contents of the book and the way in which the contributions work together. At the risk of a certain repetitiveness, I have left each contributor's general statement about aims more or less untouched. In spite of differences in structure and terminology, they overlap considerably. This will probably seem unexceptional to anybody who is unaware of the excessive degree of specialization in secondary education. It is, however, entirely hopeful and remarkable. The area of common ground between art and handicraft (wood and metalwork) is growing every day, even to the extent of the building of combined facilities in some new schools (see page 29). So I have allowed the statements to remain as a reminder of the broad background to design studies in schools and as an altogether necessary demonstration of common purpose.

In 1967 we organized, in the Department of Education Studies at Hornsey College of Art, a one-term course in Design Education for teachers from secondary schools. There were about twenty of them (art and handicraft teachers), drawn from all over Britain, and they proved to be united by a common aim to overcome their preconceptions and to revitalize their teaching by making it more directly connected with today's problems. At the end of the course we had a series of discussions and one very experienced handicraft teacher said: 'We can't make too glib claims for what we are doing. Other subject teachers are working in the same direction and some have got a good deal further than we have. Our attitude is right, I think, but our contribution has got to be just a part of a genuinely modern educational programme.' I have tried to remember that caution ever since. Although this book sets out to make some fairly big claims and to record what are real advances, the setting is the development of a total, broadly based and well-balanced curriculum.

Terminology

The idea of design studies in schools has a number of sources and, because of this, there is some confusion about terminology and where such studies fit in the pattern of general education. Particularly there is confusion between *visual* and *design* education. Visual education overlaps both art and design studies, but design studies in their turn overlap subjects like applied science where the visual/aesthetic content may be very small.

An alternative breakdown would be to speak of 'construction' and 'communication'. Construction would range from applied science through technology, engineering, building design and product design to sculpture, while communication would start from painting and run through the whole range of visual, verbal and written communication. This would be a coherent system and is, for example, used at the West of England College of Art. However, it is not generally used in schools and in the following contributions the authors' own terminology is, in the main, left untouched.

The common assumption, however diverse the terminology, is that design studies are specifically orientated towards the physical and communications problems of a world dependent on mass production and mass media, and include the environmental and communications aspects of aesthetics.

Design Education in Practice

2 IN SEARCH OF AN ALTERNATIVE ROAD

JOHN C. KINGSLAND C.B.E., B.A.

The idea of the validity of practical education has a long history, but it is only recently that it has begun to achieve the importance it deserves. In this contribution, John C Kingsland, retired headmaster of the Cray Valley Technical High School, draws on his own experiences to describe the origins of the 'alternative road' and the way it can work out in practice.

Charles Hoole, writing on education in the seventeenth century, warned schoolmasters against complacency. He wrote: 'Though every man liketh his own method best, yet ought none to be so far conceited of his own, as not to search after a better for the profiting of his scholars.' If he were living today he could scarcely complain of complacency, for never can education have been in a greater ferment. The whole administrative pattern, the content of syllabuses and the methods of teaching almost every subject are in process of major change. New mathematics, Nuffield science, audio-visual language teaching, Newsom schemes of work and Mode Three examinations are just some of the indications of educational re-thinking. A significant direction, evident in many of these changes, is towards more practical forms of education than those which have hitherto dominated the systems of Europe, and of Britain in particular.

Two inter-related problems appear to face the schools. One is to find for each pupil the kind of education that will enable him to enjoy developing to the full his potentialities, and to feel at home in a society increasingly influenced by changes in technology. The second problem is a national one. Britain has to ensure that in a highly competitive, complex and fast-changing world she has the supply of intellectual ability needed to design, to make, to distribute, to organize and to administer which modern life demands. No one form of education is likely to solve these problems.

Other countries, of course, face similar difficulties. In an interesting book from France, *L'explosion scolaire*,[1] Louis Cros shows how the emphasis, at first on the primary producer who won wealth directly from land and sea, shifted to the secondary producer who by processing primary products in factories produced vast wealth in the form of manufactured goods. The emphasis has now shifted to a third group. The specialists produce nothing directly themselves, but by their expertise in research, design, development and the use of new techniques, they rapidly increase wealth, speed communication, prolong life and open the way to a fuller and richer experience for all. Cros quotes statistics which dramatically show that it is in this third group that the shortage of man-power now lies. To make it good, we have so to reform our educational system as to make it possible to upgrade the whole of our working population, enabling larger numbers to master new techniques, to understand their changing environment, and to want to play a responsible part in controlling it. By devising a variety of congenial educational roads, with lanes for fast and slow traffic, we have to ensure that every pupil has the opportunity to travel to his limit. We are as yet only in a very early stage of creating this new system of educational roads, and traditional attitudes are delaying its construction.

At the end of the last century education beyond the elementary stage was available to only a small minority, either in independent public boarding schools or in endowed day grammar schools. The best of these schools had high standards of scholarship based upon a classical, literary curriculum, and paid great attention to character-building. Towards the end of the century it was felt that, excellent though these schools were, they were both too few in number and unsuitable in kind to meet the needs of citizens in an industrial society engaged in international trade. As early as 1882 a royal commission emphasized that higher technical education could not be developed to meet the country's needs except upon a foundation of up-to-date secondary education which included science and modern studies. Again in 1894 the Bryce Commission, set up to find the best method of establishing a well-organized system of secondary education, included in its recommendation the provision of technical secondary schools. Yet, when in 1902 an act provided for the development of secondary education, it was a somewhat modernized form of the public and endowed grammar school that became the model for the new state secondary (called county) schools. No provision for technical schools was included, and an opportunity to establish parallel types of school, one academic and the other more practical in outlook, was lost.

The county schools have become our state grammar schools, which have made a distinguished contribution to our national life in the past fifty years, and have provided opportunities so good that their aims and methods have been too readily imitated and used for those for whom they are often not suitable. Secondary technical schools on the other hand appeared more slowly and in a haphazard fashion. They were few in number, unevenly distributed and of very varying nature. Not until 1913 were regulations made for their development, and then they were treated not as part of the secondary branch of education, but were included under further education with technical and art colleges of which they were often junior departments.

They usually admitted, at 13, pupils who had failed to gain admission to grammar schools at 11, and provided for them courses with a strong vocational bias. Teaching was usually by college staff, using college equipment and thinking in terms of national certificate courses as the almost certain next step for the potential apprentices they were teaching. As a result the work had, on the one hand, an adult realism and purpose, and on the other, a rather narrow outlook and predetermined end.

Since these schools were a second choice, they smacked of the second-rate in the minds of parents, reinforcing the prevalent inclination to regard the practical as inferior to the academic. This attitude was roundly condemned in a Reith Lecture by Sir Edward Appleton when he said:

'A curious characteristic of the British has been this, that while earning our living by trade and manufacture in the past, we have at the same time affected a certain disdain of the useful and the practical. To regard anything useful as a lapse from good taste is not an attitude we should approve any more than it is an attitude we can afford. It is of little use strengthening our university departments for teaching research in the applied sciences if such work is to be regarded as second-rate activity. In the field of education we cannot allow ourselves to be betrayed into discrimination of this sort. There is more than one road to intellectual salvation.'

Yet nationally we have been, and to a large extent still are, prejudiced in favour of one road, the academic road, though this is probably suitable for only a minority. The Crowther Report,[2] published in 1954, stated: 'An observer of English education can hardly fail to be disturbed by the large number of able boys and girls who lose their intellectual curiosity before they have exhausted their capacity to learn. There are, of course, dull patches in every subject but the distaste to which we refer goes much deeper than this temporary boredom. It is more akin to *accidie*, that deep-seated apathy which theologians class as one of the seven deadly sins. They may go on working; but it will be more for what they can get out of it than for what they find in it. Is this inevitable? Where so many patently lose interest in developing powers they undoubtedly possess, and in which they used to delight, it seems that the fault must, in part at least, lie in the kind of education they are offered. We cannot afford to do without their talent.'

Teaching in a grammar school, I met this apathy and shared in experiments to find a means of countering it. These involved the introduction of more practical work and more research on contemporary problems. We found it essential to start from something familiar and real in the boy's own lives, to base real problems upon it, and to challenge them to search for a solution using their own powers of analysis and synthesis. They previously had been passive listeners and watchers, rather than active participators. They responded to this challenge, and although the work was still too academic to be of maximum interest to them, it demonstrated the truth of the adage:

I hear and I forget
I see and I remember
I do and I understand.

When I left grammar school teaching, my life and outlook underwent a considerable change. I became responsible for a combined junior technical school and junior art department, which provided vocational courses in engineering, building, and art, together with a general education. A considerable amount of time was devoted to practical work in art and crafts. This was a revealing experience, for here I found boys, without the stimulus of any external examination, working with zest and purpose particularly at the practical subjects. The urge was only partly vocational. The work clearly had intrinsic interest. It was real, like the work of the world outside. It involved active, individual participation. It developed skills in which boys could see and rejoice in their growing mastery. Because the school was closely linked to technical and art colleges and was served by their staffs, and because through them there were close links with industry, the life and work of the school formed part of the life of adult society and was seen by the boys to do so. As a result they showed a mature and responsible attitude and a pleasing confidence.

While I recognized how good much of this work was, I felt that, taken as a whole, the school experience which these boys received had shortcomings as a full education. A good deal more value might be extracted from workshop activities, which seemed to involve too little hard thinking and initiative. The boy worked his way through a carefully devised series of jobs which taught him a variety of skills, but they were set pieces, designed, thought out, blue-printed by the teacher. Boys made excellent callipers, depth gauges and adjustable squares, but they did not use them. They were not, as far as they knew, the answer to any problem. In the building course, boys built walls and knocked them down, made parts of doors and window-frames, decorated panels and cleaned them off. All the work, well done under careful instruction, was without context. The things boys made solved no problem. There was no challenge to think either why or how. Shape, size, construction, materials, tools, processes were all taken for granted, and as a result much of the educational value of the work was lost. There was little connexion between the crafts and the technical drawing intended to be the language of expression. There was only slight and intermittent cross-reference between the crafts and the science and mathematics which underpinned them.

The concept of engineering was limited to workshop practice, and of building to the practice of the crafts. The arts subjects appeared to receive scant attention and to enjoy little prestige. For some boys there was no music, art, or dramatic work at all.

I happened to read the biography[3] of Dr Sanderson, the headmaster of Oundle School, at this time, and was impressed by the way in which he had succeeded in incorporating (in the life of a public school) an ambitious programme of engineering, without sacrificing traditional studies and activities. I could see no reason why it should not be possible to do likewise in a day school. If only the zest for practical activities could be carried over into the rest of the work; if only craft subjects could be given more intellectual bite, by demanding more thought, curiosity and inventiveness! The crafts needed to be more obviously related to the courses in science and mathematics; they needed to give rise to purposeful talking and writing. Workshop interests could open windows on to a wider world, both in space and in time – they could become a powerful and liberal education which, because of strong motivation, could help some boys who seemed almost predestined for a particular kind and level of career, to reach more ambitious heights.

I had the good fortune at this time to work in contact with a number of stimulating people who were advocating or experimenting with alternative roads. Mr John Cole, Principal of the Beckenham School of Art, convinced me that a full education could be based upon art and particularly upon the teaching of design. Dr Frazer, headmaster of the progressive, long-established and highly successful Gateway School at Leicester, powerfully advocated the rehabilitation of the word 'practical' in education, and showed how such interest could become the basis of a liberal, exacting and exciting education, of great value to society and the individual. Other heads of technical schools, through meetings of local and national associations of heads, contributed to the common pool of ideas and experience from which we all freely drew. We found that though we had been working independently, in very different circumstances, we were moving in the same general direction, seeking to develop a broad but exacting education with emphasis on the ambitious use of practical activities. We were able to draw upon the help of Her Majesty's Inspectors with special interests in technical schools. Out of all this grew up the educational philosophy later described in chapter 35 of the Crowther Report under the title 'The Alternative Road'.

In my school, in working out this philosophy, I had four chief aims:

1 To break down what seemed the false and unnecessary division between general and vocational

education. I was later on delighted to read the views of Sir Handley Page on this subject. He said: 'I am not one of those who believe that you can divide education and training into vocational and non-vocational. In my view, we must look to two things – the life of man as a responsible human being and as a member of society, and we must look to his competence in some chosen field. A full personality is based equally upon a man's cultural, intellectual and spiritual life, as upon his competence in his actual occupation, be it craft, technology or management. . . We must never fall into the error of thinking that education is ever anything other than the process of development of the full man. And we can do this only if we resolve the problems of vocation and culture. It seems to me that in a healthy society, the daily vocations are part of the very fabric of the culture of the society.' At school level it seemed that we could introduce industrial techniques not in order to prepare boys for industry, but because they could provide a valuable form of education, whatever the eventual career.

2 To break down the artificial barriers between subjects, so that there was more use and illumination of one subject by another, more inter-penetration, more cross-fertilization. Specialist qualifications of teachers frequently gave rise to subject separatism.

3 To give practical subjects a greater intellectual content, by making them more provocative of thought, curiosity and invention. This could probably be achieved by involving the boy in the design aspects of making, by posing him practical problems calling for analytical and creative thinking and for personal research and investigation.

4 To let technical activities provide momentum for the whole curriculum, energizing other subjects, not only those closely related like science and mathematics, but the arts subjects also. It was plain that while some pupils – probably a minority – could be taught an abstract principle directly and later learn to apply it, there were many who could more readily and more enjoyably learn a principle by first seeing it at work, and then abstracting it for themselves. One boy can be taught verbally that the pressure of a heated gas can be made to do work in an engine cylinder. Another will more surely grasp this principle by being shown an engine at work and then challenged to find out how and why. These are different, alternative roads to learning, and both can lead to studentship of high quality.

Two experiments, begun at this time, produced interesting results. The building course included instruction in brickwork, plumbing, plastering, carpentry and joinery, painting and decorating, building construction, and the technical drawing of the industry. The craft work was limited almost entirely to the inculcation of skills. Building construction was taught rather as an end in itself than as a language for expressing ideas about the application of the crafts. Although building science and mathematics were taught with some emphasis on applications, they had little connexion with the craft courses. A young architect was appointed to teach building construction, and his influence transformed the whole course. He led boys habitually to think of a house both as a solution to the problem of comfortable and gracious living and as an important element in environment. Starting from first principles, he discussed the several functions of a house, the possible ways of fulfilling these functions in terms of size, shape, construction, materials, site, fittings and cost. Through group discussions and as individuals, boys put forward reasoned suggestions. Their whole attitude changed very markedly. Now their drawing became no longer an end in itself, but an essential means of communicating their ideas. The crafts were not merely a collection of skills, but the means whereby solutions to problems could be realized. Science and mathematics were essential bases upon which the work of the designer rested; the technology of a house depended on the application of the principles of mechanics, heat, light, sound, magnetism and electricity. Since each boy lived in a house, and houses in variety were a familiar element in the environment, he had available unlimited material for research.

The considerable momentum generated by this work quickly communicated itself to other departments, as well as those of science and mathematics. The geography course began to give special emphasis to problems of housing in different environments both at home and abroad, and to their solution in terms of available materials and techniques. The history department undertook a survey of housing through the ages, seeking to find how and why the problem of providing shelter had changed. The English department undertook to help with the preparation of written projects on these themes, while the art department helped with illustrations, organized practical experiments in interior decoration and discussed wider aspects of housing and environment.

Thus the house, the solution to a very familiar human problem, became the core of an interesting and liberal education, and the work developed on these lines led many boys, at first regarded as potential building operatives, to high qualifications and successful careers as architects and surveyors. And yet, in general, building courses have been abandoned, because the education they have provided has been too narrow and lacking in intellectual content. It is to be hoped that projects on these more imaginative lines will find their way back through Newsom schemes of work.

The second experiment reinforced the conclusions drawn from the first. One group of boys attended the art college for part of their course and were taught by a young industrial designer doing part-time teaching. Professionally he was designing and making prototype radio cabinets for mass-production. The boys became interested in this project and were invited to ask questions and offer criticisms and suggestions. They responded readily, and such was the interest that it was decided to set up a design course for them. All kinds of familiar practical problems were put before them – cooking, eating and storing food, having meals by the fire or in bed, fastening doors, windows and gates, gardening when physically handicapped, ventilating a room or a greenhouse. Starting from first principles, boys were challenged to reason their way to the solution of one of these problems. Materials of many kinds were made available – timber, metal, plastics, card, fabric, wire, nails, glue, plaster and cement, and a simply-equipped workshop was put at their disposal. Boys were encouraged to think all around the problem – function, size, shape, setting, possible materials and processes, cost, finish, and to work out a solution which would be efficient, durable and attractive in appearance.

The need to experiment with materials to discover their properties soon arose and the laboratories were called into use. A technical reference library became essential. Letters and visits to factories produced useful information and a feeling of being engaged on a real industrial enterprise.

Boys worked in their own way. Some preferred to do all their preliminary thinking on paper, producing sketches, notes and references. Others felt their way to a solution through the materials themselves. However they worked, they were required to give reasons for what they were doing and to provide a case-history of progress and findings. Boys took home the solution they had made for tests in use, and later brought their products for evaluation and critical assessment. The quality and success of the products varied greatly, but much was learnt from both failure and success. They worked with a new zest and with an urge that came from within, devoting leisure as well as class time to their projects. They gained a wide and sound knowledge of tools and materials, and confidence in knowing where to seek for information. They became critically aware and appreciative of the things around them at school, in the street, at home and in the shops. They became aware of the man-made environment. They had found a congenial road to self-development, a practical road which nevertheless encouraged them to become students. Many of these boys went on to qualify in fields originally thought to be beyond them. One won a CoID Design award. Another became a professor of industrial design. A third, whose interest in science first sprang from the unexpected behaviour of plastics, gained a university scholarship in chemistry and became an industrial chemist. Many took up careers in design, advertising and exhibition display. Each had found a powerful new motivation.

These experiments left us in no doubt about the possibilities of the design-approach to making, and of the variety of interests and studies which could spring from it. Many useful contributions were made to the work by members of the staff interested in experimenting with these teaching techniques. There seemed no reason why boys should not be made aware of design principles in activities other than art and craft. A speech or a letter is, after all, intended to solve a problem of communication and a mathematician may design a solution to a problem which is crude and clumsy or elegant and sophisticated. In their own departments and in different ways the teaching staff made various contributions to the concept of design.

In 1954 we had the opportunity to found a completely new school for boys from 11 to 18: The Cray Valley Technical High School for Boys. We felt that we now knew the sort of school we wanted it to be: a school which valued both technical skills and scholarship, and used both in providing boys with an integrated school experience. It had to foster a spirit of enquiry and a delight in creative invention, and feel itself part of the contemporary world with responsibilities for its future. It seemed clear that its curriculum must embrace the three elements in our culture – the arts, the sciences and technology, accord them equal esteem and opportunity and seek to inter-relate them comprehensibly. While carrying a full range of the usual school subjects and providing opportunities for qualifying in them at O and A level, the school would not restrict itself to traditional teaching methods. It would provide for all boys substantial technical studies not as a form of training for a career, but as a normal part of their general education.

Five men who had shared in the experiments at the previous school were appointed to form the nucleus of the staff and to give the lead in trying to develop this alternative road. We inherited a school building previously used as a grammar school. While it had good classroom, laboratory and other facilities it had only a single workshop and so was not purpose-built to serve our known needs. However, we were given the opportunity to design and equip the additional practical accommodation necessary to implement the policy of the school. This important task was undertaken by the first head of the craft department, Mr I Davies, later to become one of Her Majesty's Inspectors. A designer and craftsman of high ability, he planned in detail the new activities unit as an industrial design project. The accommodation and equipment were ambitiously conceived, and comprised:

1 A large, well-equipped drawing-office and a smaller drawing-office for advanced work.
2 Two woodwork rooms, a machine room with storage racks for timber and storage space for finished work. Machines included a circular-saw, a band-saw, a planing machine and a tool-grinder.
3 An engineering workshop with lathes, milling and shaping machines, drilling machines, a brazing hearth and ample bench space.
4 A second engineering workshop, similarly equipped but with fewer machines.
5 A technical laboratory, divided into four inter-communicating sections for:
  casting and heat treatment
  materials testing, with equipment for elementary metallurgy and for tests of hardness, brittleness and tensile strength
  electro-plating and paint-spray finishing
  work on internal combustion engines. A low-speed diesel engine made possible the study of efficiency, fuel consumption and other aspects of thermodynamics. Facilities were provided for investigating cars and motor-cycles and their components.
6 The original workshop, equipped as a combined wood and metal workshop for juniors.

Mr Davies devised and developed the first schemes of work, closely relating the crafts and the technical drawing. He established a design procedure for craft work, initiated experiments in personal investigation, fostered individual projects and research and shared in jointly conceived schemes of work relating the craft courses to those in science and mathematics. His colleagues and successors, J Mathews and R Wincott, contributed further to the work he started, adding fresh interests and activities resulting from their own experience and thinking. In this way the work remained fresh and progressive, constantly developing new growth points.

We selected as our main crafts cabinet-making and engineering. In addition the art department, under the leadership of L E Walmsley, provided courses in pottery, bookcraft, lino-cutting, fabric-printing and typography. In all this work, design considerations were kept well in mind. The two major crafts were regarded as complementary. Cabinet-making dealt with problems very familiar to boys, involved tractable materials, fairly simple techniques and provided a good means of inculcating basic design concepts. Engineering, dealing with problems in which the human element is often less directly obvious, involved less tractable materials and more complex processes, but had other values.

The engineer normally works as one of a team. His work is part of the very fabric of our social and economic life. His outlook in a fast-changing world must be alert, experimental and forward-looking. He cannot design intelligently unless he fully understands the problems his customers are seeking to solve, whether they are familiar ones in this country or very different ones overseas. His practical work, much more than that of the cabinet-maker, rests upon a basis of applied chemistry, physics, and mathematics. On some occasions he needs to prompt research himself; on others he makes use of the pure research of others and applies it. He must be able to communicate his ideas, using agreed drawings in the case of other engineers and accurate verbal description in the case of laymen. Since his clients may well be foreigners, it is a help if he has some command of at least one language other than his own. The techniques he uses and the organizations to which he belongs have their roots in the past and are part of our national history. His products, whether they be large aircraft, trains, bridges and roads or smaller devices such as radio-sets, cookers and heaters used at home, form a large part of our environment, a consideration of which he should be responsibly aware.

We argued that a broadly conceived and comprehensive curriculum, with cabinet-making and

14

engineering at its core, could touch life at many points, be realistic in conception and make considerable demands upon both teachers and pupils. Moreover, it ought to be of value to any future John Citizen, whatever career he might follow.

We believed that the problem-solving procedure that is the core of design activity could, if geared to an appropriate level, provide any boy with a tremendously useful educational experience. He could analyse all the considerations involved, suggest possible solutions in terms of materials and processes available to him. If he suggested several possible solutions it would be because it is possible to vary the weight given to the different considerations, each solution being a differently balanced compromise. He would have to use his discrimination in selecting the most promising compromise before going on to actual production. In turn, he would be designer, draughtsman, technologist, craftsman, inspector and consumer. The process of making would develop not only skill and experience of materials and tools, but real intellectual effort, involving organization, research and reasoned choice.

We found that we could start boys on these lines from the time they joined the school at the age of 11. Junior boys needed a box in which to store their workshop bits and pieces. Each needed to be labelled and stored with others in a class set. Here was our first human problem. From an older boy a typical collection of bits and pieces to be stored was borrowed and displayed. The problem was posed. By class discussion and individual suggestion possible shapes and sizes were proposed and sketched on the blackboard. Labelling and stacking in class sets imposed limitations which had to be considered. Bit by bit as considerations were reconciled an agreed solution began to emerge and was accurately expressed in drawings.

In a similar way, possible methods of construction, suitable materials and the tools available for shaping were demonstrated and discussed. Possible methods of assembly, by nailing, screwing, jointing or glueing gave rise to argument, to settle which tests had to be carried out. Small groups were formed to test the time taken for each method and the relative strengths achieved. Where individual variation was possible each boy introduced his own idea, provided that he could justify it. Eventually each box was completed, painted, and labelled, and it went into regular use. Out of its production each boy had gained his first experience of design, his first contact with a range of tools and materials and his first experience of scientific testing.

During the first two years other problems involving wood and metal were tackled in a similar way – first a cutlery box to meet mother's known needs, an extension of the box technique already mastered, then simple hand tools, domestic fixtures and a toboggan. Practical work was supplemented by outside visits, films and film-strips. The individual contribution steadily increased. A diary recorded progress, technical information and relevant cuttings from catalogues and the press. The workshop windows constantly faced outwards. The use of beech provided an opportunity to look at the furniture industry which had grown up at High Wycombe, and balsa wood a link with the Amazon forests and the Kon-Tiki expedition. Copper carried boys in imagination to Katanga or the Chilean Andes. Tools were treated in a similar way, so that a whole pattern of ideas and information developed round the practical work.

From the third year, the crafts separated into cabinet-making and engineering. In cabinet-making, the work begun in the junior school continued on more ambitious lines. A whole class would be engaged in solving a common problem, each boy working out his own solution. A design technique called the 6.3.1 method was adopted to ensure that solutions were not merely imitative, but involved original thinking and discrimination. Faced with a problem, a boy first analysed considerations of purpose, position, possible materials, construction, proportion, finish and cost. He then sketched six possible solutions. From these he chose what seemed the most satisfactory, and experimented with three modifications. Of these he selected what he had reason to think was the best, made full working drawings, drew up his materials requisition and got on with the job. The many solutions to the same problem not only provoked useful discussion, but showed the boys that there is no one ideal solution. The weight given to different considerations and the compromise decided upon, much more than pure inventiveness, accounted for the differences. With a whole group attacking one problem it was possible to cover a good deal of common technological ground and so to ensure that there was a sound underlying basic body of knowledge. As boys went up the school it was possible to give individual preference freer rein. Older boys tackled individually chosen problems, making musical instruments, furniture for their own rooms, or equipment to fill a known school need.

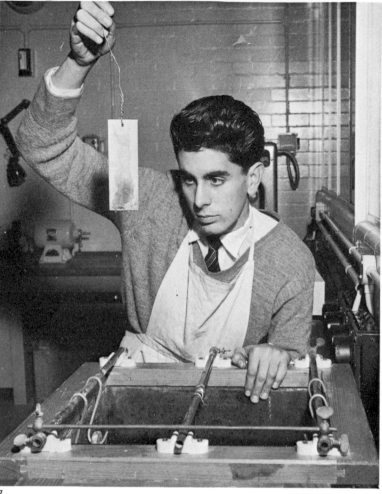

7

8

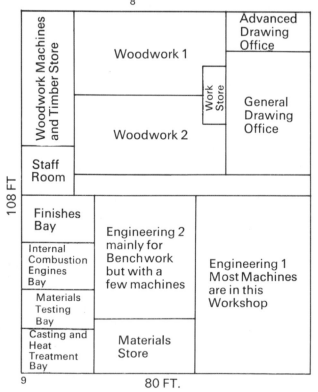

9   80 FT.

Woodwork Machines and Timber Store	Woodwork 1		Advanced Drawing Office
			General Drawing Office
	Woodwork 2	Work Store	
Staff Room			
Finishes Bay	Engineering 2 mainly for Bench work but with a few machines	Engineering 1 Most Machines are in this Workshop
Internal Combustion Engines Bay		
Materials Testing Bay		
Casting and Heat Treatment Bay	Materials Store	

108 FT

7 The 'alternative road' to education is through involvement in the practical application of knowledge. Many children find this more stimulating and realistic. Here a boy at the Cray Valley Technical High School learns about current rectification, ionization in a chemical solution and Faraday's Laws of Electrolysis by carrying out electroplating, an industrial technique to prevent the corrosion of metals.

8 Working on a motor-car chassis at the Cray Valley Technical High School. Boys learn about vehicles, but the activity is also a source of material for teaching physics and mathematics.

9 and 10 Workshops at the Cray Valley Technical High School.
9 Block plan; 10 Part of the machine shop.

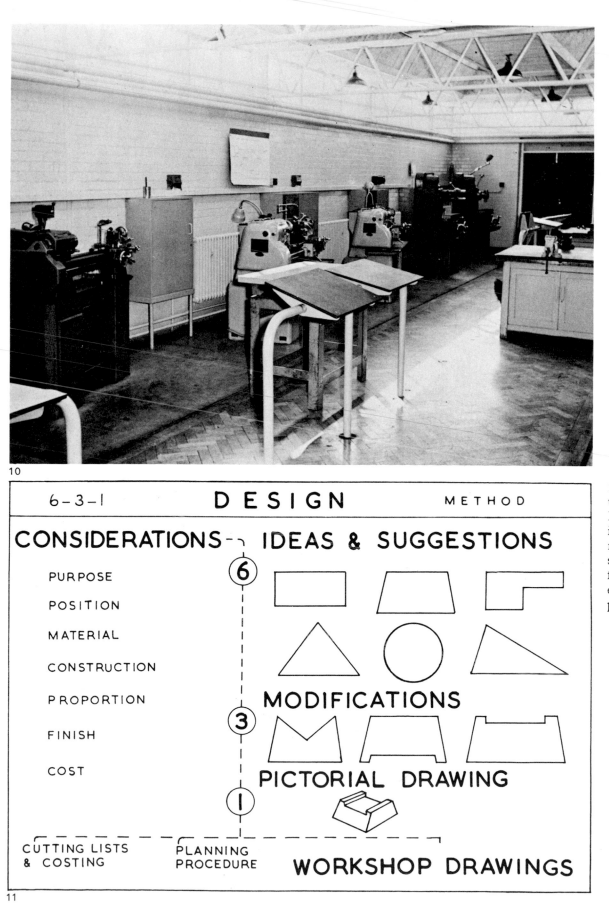

10

---

6 – 3 – 1 **D E S I G N** METHOD

CONSIDERATIONS **IDEAS & SUGGESTIONS**

PURPOSE

POSITION

MATERIAL

CONSTRUCTION

PROPORTION

FINISH

COST

6

3

MODIFICATIONS

PICTORIAL DRAWING

1

CUTTING LISTS & COSTING

PLANNING PROCEDURE

WORKSHOP DRAWINGS

11

11 Design method by selection as used at the Cray Valley Technical High School. First, up to six ideas were produced; next, the most promising of these were selected for further modification; finally, one modified design was chosen for working drawings and production.

On the engineering side, a similar but modified method was adopted. There were more difficulties here in using the design approach. Engineering materials and techniques are more complex; the problems that engineering seeks to solve lie less within the scope of the boy's experience and competence than is the case with cabinet-making. A boy cannot be expected to design intelligently unless he is well acquainted with the materials and processes which are available. It has been usual to put boys through a rather dull basic course designed to give the needed experience. It is hardly to be expected that a boy will be much motivated by the process of making a set-spanner by hand, even though it may develop skill. The wider implications and educational content of such a product are also limited. We found, however, that even with such a simple tool the boy could be made aware of the problem he was attempting to solve and be taken through the design factors which affect the result. Added interest to the work could also be given, if the making process was accompanied by a practical and scientific study of the behaviour of the metals employed. In this way the foundations of a technological approach were laid. It proved to be helpful if boys could make something which more obviously worked, for the desire to complete a working device carried them through the practice of skills, and the intellectual content of a working device was often greater. Devices such as electric motors, however simple, cranes or fork-lift trucks operated by inexpensive electric motors and harmonographs all proved powerful incentives to develop craft skill and open the way to experimental work in applied science.

If opportunities to stretch a boy's thinking powers through design are less obvious in engineering, there are alternatives, for boys can be challenged to think hard about ways of producing a known result. For example, a successful experiment in batch production was tried in the middle school. The teaching staff designed and made a model steam engine, involving steel, aluminium, brass and zinc alloy and showed it, working, to the boys. Each boy was keen to make one. Made individually, the engines would have taken too long, and the advantages of batch production were therefore discussed. The group was divided into teams of six boys and told that, using the resources of the workshops, each team was to produce six identical engines with interchangeable parts, the teams being in competition both for speed of completion and for quality of product.

The engine was dismantled and the parts laid out for inspection. Each group discussed methods of producing multiple castings for base and flywheel, jigs for standardized identical parts, a production procedure and an allocation of work. The work involved considerable planning and inventiveness. Problems, such as bottlenecks involved in production, were quickly met and had to be overcome. Each boy eventually assembled one engine from the parts made by his group, and then, using compressed air, engines were tested for performance and efficiency by measuring their brake horse-power. During the making boys were required to keep case histories, and to carry out in the technical laboratory a series of metallurgical tests on the materials used. Quite incidentally they gained a very practical understanding of pyrometry, coefficients of expansion and cooling curves in connexion with their casting, and of current rectification, ionization in a solution and Faraday's laws of electrolysis in providing an electro-plating finish to some of the parts. The whole of this work had the added advantage of anticipating in a very practical way the more advanced work in thermodynamics which would follow in the sixth form.

While a boy can hardly be expected to design a machine in the engineer's sense of the word, he can be led to become critically aware of the design of those he uses. He can analyse a machine, abstracting the basic principle from the many parts. He can think about ergonomic considerations involved in its use and their effect on design. Again he can see that design is usually a matter of compromise. As Professor Brosan says: 'With a problem defined, there may be several solutions. There may or may not be large amounts of originality involved, but some will always be present. A real engineering problem will not be best dealt with by applying a formula. The synthesis leading to a solution may well cut across the formal academic fields of study. A student should be led to realize that there is no one solution to an engineering problem; rather there are a number of solutions – perhaps a best one – which must be arrived at by discrimination.'

The Crowther Report queried whether the practical approach could provide a severe enough intellectual challenge for sixth forms and concluded that the technical schools had shown that it could. We had certainly found that at sixth-form level, practical work could become very exacting and truly technological in nature. We tried a variety of approaches. All boys in the sixth, whatever their A-level courses, included technical studies in their curriculum. Some boys undertook individual technical projects arising from aspects of their A-level work in chemistry, physics or applied mathematics. Some of the work was constructional, boys building telescopes, photographic enlargers, go-karts, hovercraft, radio-controlled cars, ships or aircraft, musical instruments and electronic devices, including a computer. Other work was of a research nature, boys devising means of comparing the lubricating qualities of brands of oil, or the relative lasting power of electro-plating and paint spray finishes. Often work which started on a constructional basis quickly involved research and experiment. When two boys decided to make a wind tunnel in order to find an ideal shape for a special car body, they soon found themselves so deeply involved that they spent some time in a university aeronautical laboratory acquiring the necessary background.

We experimented with short courses in metallurgy, thermodynamics, structures, and electronics, to which we would gladly have added hydraulics, had it been possible. What we could offer depended upon what existing members of the staff could provide, or what help we could obtain from university, technical college, or industry. Out of the short courses, which gave all boys something to bite on, projects arose in a definite context, and some of these proved invaluable. From a course on structures and an associated visit to the new Medway bridge then under construction, a series of experiments on reinforced and pre-stressed concrete beams developed. Out of these again arose a keenly contested competition in bridge design. Boys were asked to design in not more than two ounces of balsa wood a bridge to span a twelve-inch gap seeking to obtain the maximum load/weight ratio. Over eighty entries in great variety of design were submitted and tested to destruction, the provision of acceptable scientific methods of testing providing a further challenge to ingenuity.

In recent years this kind of work under a variety of names – engineering, technology, applied science, technical activities – has been developing in schools of all kinds. In some schools it is a voluntary out-of-class activity for boys working on academic A-level courses. In others it has developed either as a main A-level course or in the same way that sixth-form general studies have developed. Sometimes school science departments have fostered practical applied science to supplement and illuminate A-level science. Some schools, working with technical colleges, have set up engineering courses to give sixth formers a greater understanding of the real nature and scope of engineering. In 1965, at the invitation of the Institute of Mechanical Engineers, Mr G T Page undertook a survey of 290 schools in order to find out the nature and scope of the technical work then going on. His findings were published in a report entitled *Engineering among the Schools*.[4] It revealed the wide range of work in progress, described the effect of the work on advanced level studies, its purely educational value and its influence on attitudes towards engineering as a career. It also gave details of the methods being tried to assess the work, and attempts made to gain recognition for it as an A-level study, acceptable for university entrance.

At about the same time, Mr D I R Porter, HMI, as Simon Senior Research Fellow at Manchester University, was undertaking an enquiry on the approach to technology in the schools. In 1967 the Schools Council published his report under the title *A School Approach to Technology*.[5] This report placed practical activities in their historical perspective, showed their significance against the present social, economic and educational background, described a variety of alternative educational roads involving practical activities and concluded by making stimulating suggestions as to how schools might further develop linked courses in science, mathematics and the crafts at different age levels.

The two reports are in many ways complementary, and appeared at a most appropriate time when many schools developing technical studies felt that they were working in isolation, while others, wishing to begin, needed information on how to proceed. The Schools Council has taken a valuable initiative in setting up *Project Technology*, in which grouped schools and associated colleges exchange and disseminate ideas. Experiments in technology are being studied as to their suitability for wider application. It is hoped that interest will spread outwards from schools already in the project, and that in this way practical activities as the Crowther Report envisaged them will be more fully developed in schools of all kinds. At least the need is now fully recognized.

It needs stressing that the alternative road is not an easier road than the academic one, but that it is different. A curriculum with technical activities at its core can motivate pupils to stretch their intellectual powers, use their imagination, co-ordinate their studies and foster their skills in an atmosphere of contemporary realism. It can thus produce students of high calibre. The nature of the road need not predetermine the destination. What is important is that every pupil should find himself on a road so congenial that he retains his zest to go on travelling.

To live fully and intelligently in modern society it is necessary to have a philosophy which takes technology into account. In the past the simple technologies of the farmer, builder, wheelwright and blacksmith were familiar to all. Children grew up in close touch with them, and unconsciously absorbed them. This simple technology was an integral part of the culture of the community. The increase in range and complexity of modern technology has changed all this. Children grow up in a world of sealed units, little black boxes and mysterious goings-on in factories guarded by security officers. Even modern buildings arriving in prefabricated units are assembled behind a screen of shuttering, while the family car disappears for servicing into the workshops behind the garage fore-court to be operated on in secret. We cannot absorb technology as part of our culture. It mystifies and frightens us, threatening to dominate our lives and possibly to destroy us. We are inclined to think of it as a kind of package deal that we must accept in its entirety. If we want research to provide life-prolonging antibiotics, we feel that we must also accept germ warfare; if we want electric power from nuclear fission we must also risk death from the nuclear bomb.

Much of our present malaise springs from the disintegration of our culture. The arts, the sciences and technology move farther apart. So great is the degree of specialization that we may well have real contact with only one of these elements though having to make important decisions – in ignorance – involving the others. It is a matter of urgency that we find the means of re-integrating our culture. Since this involves re-education it is at school level that the task must begin. An education for today must include the arts, the sciences and technology, so brought together that they constitute a comprehensible, unified experience. Technology must be seen as a man-centred, man-directed activity, capable of solving human problems and making possible a fuller, more pleasant life for all mankind. But human values have first to be established, and moral choice exerted to ensure that men use technology to promote human welfare, improve health, increase wealth, eliminate drudgery and make available more leisure and the means of using it in satisfying ways.

The alternative road, providing as it does a balanced curriculum compounded of the three elements in our contemporary culture, is admirably suited to meet the needs of modern society and of the individual in that society.

[1] LOUIS CROS. English translation: *Explosion in the Schools*. Parker & Sons (1961).
[2] *15 to 18*, the Crowther Report. Ministry of Education, Central Advisory Council for Education (England). H.M.S.O. (1959).
[3] *Sanderson of Oundle*. Memorial Volume (1923).
[4] G. T. PAGE. *Engineering among the Schools*. The Institute of Mechanical Engineers (1965).
[5] D. I. R. PORTER. A School Approach to Technology. *Schools Council Curriculum Bulletin No.2*. H.M.S.O. (1967).

Design Education in Practice

3   SCHOOL WORKSHOPS

BERNARD J. AYLWARD

Bernard J. Aylward is Handicraft Adviser to the Leicestershire Education Committee. He discusses the role that school workshops, with their highly trained staff and specialist equipment, have to play in design studies. Leicestershire has for many years recognized the importance of practical education, and many of its schools are now being planned to make possible physical and educational links between handicraft, art, and homecraft.

Unless the reader is personally involved in practical education the term handicraft is likely to give quite a false impression. The name is not even universally accepted, and useful arts, industrial arts, handwork and technical subjects are all used to denote the same field of activity. It is almost impossible to find a teacher involved in it who likes the name handicraft and quite impossible to find an alternative that would be acceptable to all.

Today the range of activities becomes increasingly wide so that it is difficult to give a simple definition. Very roughly the work is concerned with the designing and making of useful things in the more permanent and resistant materials. It merges with art – another similarly vague term – at one end of the spectrum and with science at the other. In the past it has been confined almost entirely to boys, but more and more girls are being encouraged to come into the workshops. This is as it should be, and although the word 'boy' may appear in this contribution, it should not be taken to mean that girls cannot benefit from these activities.

It should be realized that there is already considerable provision for this sort of work in schools. It is supported by special expensively equipped rooms and teachers trained to use them. Fortunately they have a big part to play in the new approach to practical education that takes design as its central theme; but if design departments are to flourish, the nature of their contribution must be clearly understood.

In order to do this it is well first of all to look more closely at the activities that now take place. The emphasis on making useful things from permanent and resistant materials has had a profound influence on the whole direction of handicraft teaching. Most durable consumer products have been made of wood or metal. As a result handicraft has concentrated on these materials and rooms are most often equipped exclusively for one or the other. Although colleges of education have for many years given student handicraft teachers experience in both, most of them will have specialized to some extent in one. Yet the variety of new materials available today means that one of the first things a designer must do – after he has identified the problem facing him – is to decide on the most suitable material to use. But before we condemn handicraft for sticking to a limited range we ought to see if this has any educational advantages.

The first advantage seems to be that in a rapidly changing world wood and metalwork can contribute a distinctive sense of direction. This is not to suggest that change is bad, but the more we hope to adventure away from the rigid structures of society of the past, the more we need to know where we are going. Often a more reliable guide will be a knowledge of how we reached our present position from the past rather than wild guesses about a largely unknown future. To have experience of a craft that stems from the remote past, providing it is relevant to our present way of living, is an excellent way of developing such knowledge. This is a major contribution to the development of a child's experience that should not lightly be abandoned.

The second easily identified advantage lies in the teacher's likely attitude. One of the most important qualities required of a teacher is enthusiasm and it often happens that teachers are most enthusiastic about one particular craft. Many children have been led to partake in an activity which they can enjoy for a lifetime by teachers with this quality.

For these two reasons alone one must be cautious. The task should not be to replace this kind of teaching with another, but to put it in such a context that it makes more sense and becomes more relevant to life in the world that exists today.

A positive and negative factor is that to work in these materials – or any similar resistant material – demands quite advanced techniques. The positive aspect is the relationship with real-life activities – before most useful things can actually be produced someone has to use a highly developed skill, even if it is to make a machine which in turn makes the product. And it is not a bad thing if – as part of their education – children gain some appreciation of this hard fact of life. Negatively, it is the need for advanced techniques that has in the past led to an admitted over-concentration on the mere acquisition of skill. However, to remove all need for skill would be to lose much of the present value of craft education. Here again the appropriateness of the context is the key issue. Instead of trying to cut out skill, teachers are developing courses that enable children to acquire only those skills that are really essential, as quickly as possible, and in relation to projects that make the acquisition an obvious necessity to the children themselves.

It is because handicraft must be concerned with technology as well as aesthetics that it has a key role to play in design education. Nor is this such a new thing. It has been so for at least twenty years, and the best teaching in that time has always challenged children to design their own work. That much of it was still hackneyed must be admitted. Children of a society uninterested in good design, working within a traditional framework, using a limited range of materials and aiming at a traditional solution are hardly likely to produce anything of startling originality. Some of these factors, beyond the control of the school, are likely to be a brake on progress for some time, but at least it is now possible to make a clear statement, based to some extent on experience, of the role of the school workshops in design education.

When children are involved in the process of design it is essential that they should be allowed to think radically and not simply accept the standard solution to a problem. They need to be able to look with a fresh vision at problems and be alert to take advantage of anything new that will really make for a better solution. They need to be capable of discrimination so as to avoid facile assumptions. A lot of this kind of experience can best be obtained practically in the workshop. In working out designs there is a place for mock-ups, hammer-and-nail versions of products to be made in other materials, plaster models – all the quick simulation techniques that make it possible to study *three-dimensionally* the function and appearance of an object before beginning its production.

This is, however, only a part of the story. Design studies that dealt only in these terms would lack the bite of reality. The test of a design is not only related to its concept, but to the realization of that concept. The designer has to have a language with which to communicate and a good knowledge of methods of making.

Children working on design problems can find in the technical drawing aspect of handicraft an aid to clear thinking, and a bridge between mock-up and reality. Unfortunately the subject has suffered more than most by the way it has been mis-handled in syllabuses and examinations. Often it becomes little more than the acquisition of skill in using instruments and a knowledge of often out-dated machine parts. But, at best, it is already taught as the graphic expression of the designer. In this role it can organize and clarify original concepts into clearly defined designs that can satisfactorily be produced.

The last stage is the making of the designed product. Educationally this has very great importance involving, as it does, an encounter with the standards and requirements of the adult world. The ease with which mock-ups and simulations are made can be a serious trap, for illusion is useless for a real product. A chair must not only appear to support a body; it must in fact do so. Without this final stage of realization, design can hardly be said to exist. The proof of the pudding is in the eating and the proof of the design is in the using of the finally made product. It is here that many of the long-held tenets of handicraft teaching – craftsmanship, skill, sound construction – find a real relevance and meaning in the experience of the child.

Having examined the relevance of the work done in handicraft departments, it becomes possible to consider the sort of course that can and should be established today. Many teachers have for some time been trying out all kinds of ideas, and by now it is possible to devise a progressive and satisfactory course. What is needed instead of a list of things to make is a series of experiences. These should seek to arouse a child's interest in materials and in making things, and should help to cultivate the understanding eye which is essential if he is going to appraise critically his own environment. Too often in the past crafts teaching confined itself merely to developing an interest in making things.

Is it possible to devise a way of teaching that will enable those for whom it is appropriate to acquire

12

14

13

12 Metalwork in a Leicestershire school.
13 The manufacture of most industrial products depends at some stage on the exercise of skill in using machinery. It is a valuable educational experience if children learn something of the techniques, limitations and opportunities involved while they are at school.
14 Working in wood and metal brings children into contact with the standards and requirements of the adult world.

a craft skill, and yet give others a valuable educational experience? I believe that many teachers, by arousing the children's interest in materials and helping them to cultivate an understanding eye, as well as teaching them some skill, are showing that it can.

Such a course might well start with some experience of materials as materials, and this ought to take place in the primary school. Those early years are the age of exploration and much is already done to give children a wide range of experiences. Unfortunately the range nearly always stops short of wood and metal. This is very understandable since most primary schools lack accommodation, equipment, the necessary money, or teachers with sufficient confidence in handling these materials. Above all the need to occupy classes of forty or more in one classroom makes the development of work in wood and metal somewhat hazardous. It is not suggested for one moment that formal handicraft teaching should be introduced into primary schools. But only a minimum of facilities are necessary if children are to use these materials; and teachers do not have to be expert craftsmen – all they need is sufficient confidence themselves to inspire confidence in their pupils. If these conditions are available there is a wide range of work possible for the limited strength of primary-school children and the simple facilities that could be available (see illustrations 15 and 17).

It is often worth while when looking for suitable work to think of the way primitive man fulfilled his needs, since he also had to do so with very limited equipment. This would have the added advantage of appealing to the imagination of the children and linking up with their investigations of geography and early history. One of the earliest ways of working metal was by casting, and although the sort done in the secondary school would be inappropriate, it is easy to melt lead or one of the zinc-based alloys over a gas flame in an iron ladle. This could be done with great satisfaction by primary-school children, and there is no reason why it should be dangerous.

Primitive man found that the easiest way to join wood was by boring a hole and fitting a peg into it. Dowels and a brace and bit could give a boy a way of construction that would allow him to make quite a lot of things. Primitive carving with gouge and mallet is far safer than many would think if a bench and vice is provided so that the wood can be firmly held and both hands occupied with the tool. Copper and brass wire and thin sheet can be cut, bent, twisted and joined with soft solder to allow boys to produce a lot of useful things. Those familiar with craft teaching in a primary school may well be dubious about the wisdom of some of these suggestions. Although the difficulties already mentioned have to be overcome before tackling such work, given suitable conditions it can be done. The suggestions are made from personal experience of small groups in primary schools who did all these things.

15

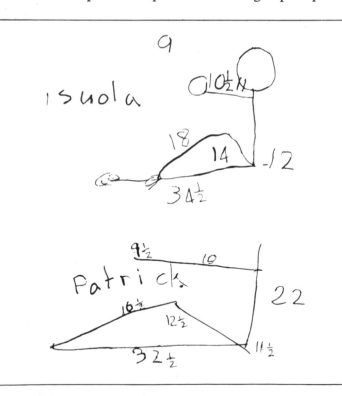

16

15 and 16 There is no reason why a start on design studies should not be made in primary schools. Shown here are a chair made by 9- and 10-year-olds at Medbourne School, Leicestershire using traditional methods like riving, splitting and rounding, and diagrams of human dimensions made by children in a London primary school.

17

18

17–19 Certain kinds of exploratory work are valid at a variety of levels. Finding out about the capacity and character of materials is an area where the school workshops play a constantly developing role in design studies. 17 Shows simple shaping work in a primary school; 18 Shows shaping related to a particular range of techniques carried out early in the secondary school; 19 Shows sophisticated joining exercises by students at Cardiff College of Art.

19

Since conditions in most primary schools, however, are not conducive to encouraging this kind of experience, it will be necessary to give opportunity for it in secondary schools; but in the time available it just will not be possible to let pupils spend too long on this stage. Also many will want to tackle some real problem in a more mature way. Hence it would be well to present such explorations as specific problems. The children, given a piece of rough wood, can be asked to make it fit smoothly into the hand, or make it into a specified kind of shape. Some teachers have found that children brought up on science-fiction jargon will even cope with the demand to make it visually arresting. It might be topical, if archaeology was in the news, to suggest shaping a piece of material so that if found in the earth it would be recognized as having been worked by man. This amount of direction will make their efforts more effective. Those who lack imagination or even application may well be encouraged and all will be able to exercise some judgement as to their own success in achieving a desired result. They will also have found out at first hand something of the nature and fascination of wood. Similar experiences can be devised for metal.

Teachers developing this kind of work have to be encouraging and permissive so that pupils are allowed a genuine sense of discovery. The aim is to arouse a fascination for the material and to give only as much guidance as necessary. The children must be left to find out for themselves. Teachers will also be alert for signs of boredom and face the sad fact that many children are not as curious as they should be, and are only too ready to be told what to do. Further stimulus must then be given by showing other things that can be done. This might take the form of showing how certain tools are used or certain processes carried out. It is then possible to use these tools and processes to make interesting shapes or forms or even small articles that can be used or enjoyed.

There must be a sense of progression in any good course and both pupils and teachers should be aware of a growing mastery. This is so often missing, and pupils, having spent some time enjoying a material, are then plunged straight into a formal course. If they are to get the best from a course they should see the later work developing naturally from the earlier. Hence the way in which the next sort of experience is presented to them is of vital importance. If progress is to be made the experience must be sufficiently organized to add to a boy's skill and understanding. Yet if it is to stimulate his curiosity, it must not be too restrictively defined. The extent to which the work can give scope for personal choice is one of the most difficult decisions for the teacher to make. Children should never be allowed to become lost in a situation beyond their capacity, but equally they should have to exercise discrimination.

Some teachers have found that a useful next step is to suggest using known tools and processes to produce structures with specific qualities – for example, height, lightness, or strength. It will give more practice in the use of tools, together with the further demands of joining materials. Since construction is necessary for any advance towards the mastery of a craft, this will be seen to be real progress. Moreover it will offer a challenge to consider simple spatial relations and a chance of success at various levels. This last point is important since a simple pass/fail situation with the scales heavily weighted on the side of failure is not likely to encourage interest or progress.

From such an experience it will be possible to move on to the beginnings of the design process. The children could first be asked to make some small article for their own use. They might still need help over choice of material and ways of working it. In fact faced with a specific need, good direct teaching of a technique with demonstration and practice might well be appropriate and welcome.

One parameter of design that they should be able to cope with is function. Many of the small jobs made at the beginning of the earlier more formal courses can be presented as problems in function: the important factor is the method of presentation rather than the actual job made. Quite ordinary things may be made in quite an ordinary way, but the quality of thinking demanded may be of a very high order.

The most important experience that the child should have is the realization that handicraft involves the making of decisions. The understanding that everything that is made must first be designed is the first step in understanding design itself. The speed and extent to which children can be led on to tackle more complex design problems will again depend on many factors. The amount of time spent in the craft department, the ability of the boys and their home background will be the most important, and the success of the course will depend on the skill of the teacher in matching his demands to the capacity of the children. His aim should be to get as many pupils, as soon as possible, deciding on their own problems and how to solve them.

It may have to be faced that in certain specific circumstances some boys will never, in any real sense, design their own jobs. There may be little desire to think of anything to make since there is no habit in their homes of seeking to improve its comfort, convenience, or beauty. If in order to succeed they need detailed instruction and no demands on their limited capacity to make decisions, then it is initially at least the job of the handicraft department to give them this opportunity. Yet they too can enjoy cutting, shaping, or even just bashing material and as a start this can prove worth while. Large branches or old telegraph posts that can be made into fantastic totem poles have often been found easier to manage than small pieces of material needing greater precision in handling. To be able to make some simple thing (for a local hospital or old-age pensioner if mum and dad do not want it) by assembling ready-made parts might be a starting point. Without a starting point nothing is possible; but once started a boy can be expected to progress. Progress is often more possible by the use of machines than the learning of very demanding skills. One teacher is having some success in getting students of little ability to make design decisions, by allowing them to base their work almost entirely on simple machine jigs. In doing so they produce something that is in some measure their own design, and gain the beginnings of an understanding of the thought process involved.

At the other end of the ability range there seems no doubt that the goal is a full experience of design decision-making with the practical workshops at the core of the activity. Able sixth-formers in certain schools are already tackling real engineering problems of some complexity, and the theme of the inter-relation of practical work and intellectual development can be found in all the contributions to this book. Once again it is the context that can give to craft skills and activity their proper educational role.

Often advanced studies at sixth-form level are done outside the examination structure and this means that there is inevitably a limit on their support and further development. However, some examining boards are accepting syllabuses in engineering that demand a genuine problem-solving approach. Now the Oxford Delegacy has accepted an A-level syllabus in design developed in Leicestershire by a working party of teachers and designers. The object of this exercise is to define a field of study in such a way as to demonstrate the possibility of organizing a sixth-form course which will make the students aware of the importance of design to mankind and help them gain some understanding of the nature of the design process. It should also show that it can be sufficiently demanding intellectually to sustain a course at sixth-form level.

In addition to engaging in a design project which will have to be assessed, students will undertake a course of study under three headings. One will be that of *Man as an individual* which will seek to give them sufficient knowledge of the sizes, shapes, limitations, and needs of man to think sensibly about articles for man's use. A section on *Man in society* will deal with the organization of commerce. The third section will be on technology; and so that this vast subject shall not be overwhelming, a student will be expected to gain a general understanding of all the materials now at the disposal of the designer, but study in some depth only one section within which the main part of his project will fall.

This is not in any sense the full answer to design education even at sixth-form level, and one must be alert to the danger of isolating design as a separate subject to be studied only by a few. One headmaster connected with the study of the design syllabus has already said that he would like to arrange such a course – but not to the same level nor in order to pass an examination – for the whole of his sixth form. Certainly unless we reach a stage when it is impossible to be considered a cultured person without some appreciation of the design process and a cultivated interest in the visual world, there is little hope of developing civilization and a beautiful environment.

Cost is a problem which has to be faced in introducing design studies. It is involved in both the materials and time used to produce the objects which have been designed. In the past this has often led to safe and humdrum efforts, and one must have sympathy with children who are unwilling to risk so much effort and cash on something which may be unsatisfactory in the end. To allow a budding craftsman to spend six months or more on a piece of work that is bound to fail is not going to develop an interest in a craft or in design. It is here that proper design methodology is so important, for it is only when there has been the opportunity to sketch, to try out mock-ups in easily worked materials, to use laboratory facilities to test materials and construction that there can be reasonable certainty of success.

Cost is also bound up with facilities, but it should not be argued that lack of facilities make design

20–22 Exploration of the technical and aesthetic potential of materials carried out by students of Cardiff College of Art.

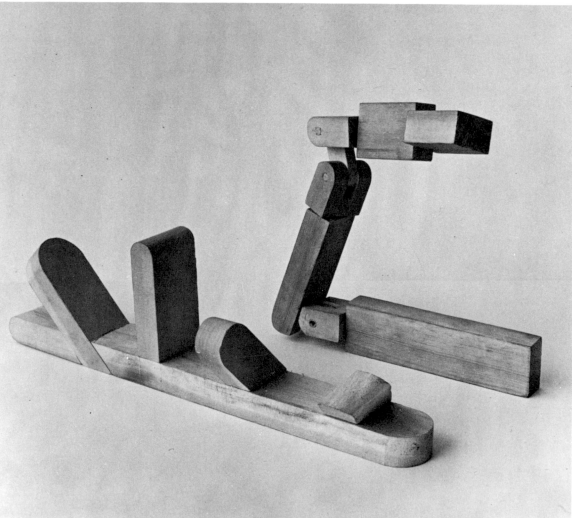

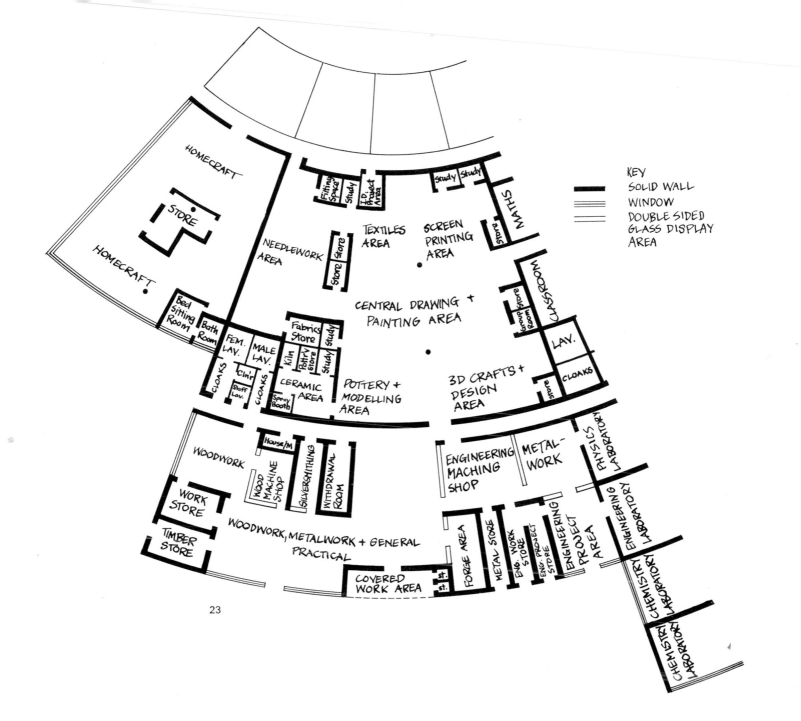

Within the figure the following labels appear:

HOMECRAFT

STORE

HOMECRAFT

Bed Sitting Room | Bath Room

Fitting Space | Study | I.D. Project Area

Study | Study

Store | MATHS

TEXTILES AREA | SCREEN PRINTING AREA

NEEDLEWORK AREA

Store | Store

KEY
— SOLID WALL
≡ WINDOW
DOUBLE SIDED GLASS DISPLAY AREA

CENTRAL DRAWING + PAINTING AREA

CLASSROOM

Group Store Room

LAV.

FEM. LAV. | MALE LAV.

Fabrics Store

Kiln | Pottry Store | Study | Study

CLOAKS

CLOAKS | Staff Lav. | Clnr

Spray Booth

CERAMIC AREA

POTTERY + MODELLING AREA

3D CRAFTS + DESIGN AREA

Store | CLOAKS

WOODWORK

House/M

Wood Machine Shop | Silversmithing | Withdrawal Room

ENGINEERING MACHING SHOP | METAL-WORK

PHYSICS LABORATORY

WORK STORE

TIMBER STORE

WOODWORK, METALWORK + GENERAL PRACTICAL

FORGE AREA | METAL STORE | Eng. Work Store | Eng. Project Store | ENGINEERING PROJECT AREA | ENGINEERING LABORATORY

COVERED WORK AREA | St. | St.

CHEMISTRY LABORATORY | CHEMISTRY LABORATORY

23

23 Layout plan of the practical area facilities proposed at Countesthorpe School in Leicestershire. The building is circular and the linked facilities for homecraft, art and handicraft adjoin the science area which includes an engineering laboratory. Architects: Farmer and Dark in collaboration with T. A. Collins, Leicestershire county architect.

studies impossible. The industrial designer himself must be aware of the facilities at the disposal of the manufacturer if he is to be of any use. He must accept the discipline of using existing capital equipment and the demand for economy of production. Although in the school situation restrictions on freedom of design may be more severe, the need to understand the way in which an artefact can be made with the equipment and materials available is not, in principle, different from the discipline faced by the professional designer. In a small school where there may be only one or two teachers, it may well be necessary to settle for giving pupils a real understanding of, and ability to design in, a more limited range of materials than would be possible in a larger school.

When considering new provision for crafts, it is important to remember that some are better carried out in a carefully arranged environment. It is obvious, for example, that forging and fine cabinet work would not easily mix. The advantage of having the exact requirements for one craft should always be weighed against encouraging an interest in many. Ideally one would like to see plenty of general space where all sorts of activities could take place, with specialized areas where certain ones can be taken to a high standard. Illustration 23, which is a plan of Countesthorpe Upper School, Leicestershire, shows how in a large school it is possible to achieve an essential unity in a department without producing conditions in which it is difficult for craftsmanship to flourish. Some attempts to achieve integration have taken the form of vast open spaces reminiscent of aeroplane hangars. These, because they tend to reduce a human being to a cipher, are hardly the places for personal creative development. It is interesting to notice how, at Countesthorpe, the workshop areas are carefully placed in a total context involving art and homecraft and directly linked with science.

Although this contribution may appear to deal with very wide interests, all these are the rightful concern of a good crafts teacher. He may not be able from personal knowledge and experience to teach all that is involved in design – from basic understanding of form, colour, texture, etc. to the advanced technology needed to complete an engineering project – but his work is central. He must be aware of the whole problem and know when and where to seek help for his students from other members of staff or friends in industry. Just as design is the meeting place of the sciences and the humanities, so good crafts-teaching uses and enriches many aspects of learning. In doing so it can act as a unifying influence in an education that otherwise could consist of isolated bodies of knowledge lacking significance.

The product of the teaching is not the tool or the bowl, but the attitude of the boy, and this is conditioned not only by the ability of the teacher but the starting point of the boy. It is not so obvious or so easily assessed as in other school activities, so that criticism of what is done and the standard achieved should always be cautious. The more all teachers – not only those concerned with the crafts – themselves become aware of their surroundings and consider that an intelligent understanding of environment is an essential part of education, the easier it will be to make progress.

The ties are particularly strong between art and handicraft. These should work hand in glove, if possible in the same department, with maximum visual contact and only enough separation to avoid mutual discomfort from noise and dirt, and provide some space where craftsmen can develop their own individual creativity without interruption. Then the students will see that all these activities are linked; that to see with understanding is as much a part of handicraft as of art and that whereas a pretty sketch is not a design, no more is an object that crudely and inelegantly fulfils a function. The total experience that he can have in such a department can help him to look afresh at materials, to think carefully what the problem really is before he attempts to solve it, to be bold in trying quite new ideas and finally to produce something that is practical and sound, yet pleasing and fresh. If he cannot quite do that he may at least gain some knowledge whereby he can assess soundly the success with which a designer has done so. He will be a more discriminating buyer and one who demands a better environment in which to live.

Design Education in Practice

4 ART ROOMS

ANTHONY HORROCKS A.T.C.

This contribution is based on the recent work of staff and students in the Department of Education Studies at Hornsey College of Art. Its aim is to describe something of the developing pattern of ideas which provide a basis for greatly increasing the potential of art education in secondary schools. Anthony Horrocks is Senior Lecturer in the department.

The rapid industrialization and urbanization of society have given rise to dramatic changes in our way of living. Technological advance, mass production and automation provide the stem for the vast mushroom of mass consumer goods, mass housing and mass transportation. At the same time we are increasing our spending power. Mass communication methods have made possible mass advertising. Film, television, newspapers and magazines all strive to proliferate our wants. Increasing numbers of standardized products compete for markets not only by their functional efficiency, but also by the size of the extra inducements that they offer. Changes in fashion are more dictated by advertising pressure than by developing human needs.

Expansion, change and development are the themes of our industrial society. Many of its aspects are exciting and stimulating, but at the same time confusing. If we are to provide an education which will enable the individual not only to survive, but to survive well, then we must develop teaching programmes which lead to a reasoned understanding of the environment in which we all live. Through this understanding the individual will be able to change his personal, immediate situation, and collectively use the mass pressures of society to make relevant changes on a larger scale. To devise methods for increasing critical awareness of immediate surroundings, and a sense of responsibility for the total designed environment, is one of the key educational problems which society presents to the teacher.

The art teacher – an education designer

One way of looking at the role of the teacher is as an education designer. That is, he or she is responsible for solving in educational terms the problem which the clients – society and the individual – have presented. In this context, it would be right to enquire initially how well training and experience equip the teacher to provide solutions.

To generalize, it seems that until recently the specialist art teacher, drawn largely from the fine art departments of colleges of art, has been encouraged to rely mainly upon his own particular specialization, for example painting or sculpture, often with the addition of perhaps a couple of crafts like pottery or bookbinding. Through the teacher these specialist skills have come to provide the media for the educational experience of the child or young person.

The educational factors which have been the main concern have been those with which the student-teacher was involved during his specialist training – emotional and psychological development, self-expression and the ability to produce a personalized image. Definitions of art education have included such words as observation, seeing, creativity, visual literacy and visual awareness. These definitions have grown up over the years in a genuine attempt to give art-room activities a greater relevance than the mere opportunity to be a sophisticated version of playtime.

An encouraging aspect of the changing nature of art education is that it has become increasingly

31

outward looking, but when we ask the questions 'seeing what?', 'observing what?' and 'visually aware of what?' we are too often met with a generalized answer – 'the environment'.

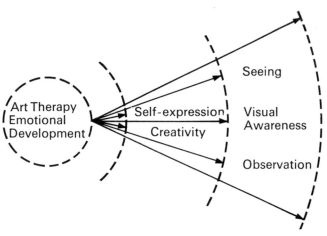

24

The problem is that the previous experience of an art student starting a postgraduate teacher-training course only provides a sound basis for designing those educational experiences that are concerned with the subjective and intuitive aspects of child development. Difficulties arise as soon as we start asking which particular aspects of the environment influence our lives to the greatest extent. The methods of approach that are valid for an attempt to encourage a generalized visual awareness become insufficient when applied to specific situations or products in the environment. In other words, it is difficult to conceive the relevance of an entirely subjective, intuitive approach to a man-made environment which has largely come about through objective, rational, decision-making processes.

This increasing awareness of the value of an art education more related to the needs of an individual in an industrial society also makes it necessary that the art teacher understands the role of other human activities. An *understanding* of, and not just a poetic *sympathy* for, the sciences, mathematics, technology, economics, methodology and planning will make the designing of genuinely relevant educational situations more possible.

Thus the art teacher has not only to develop an understanding of industrial society which will help him to identify the problem areas which are relevant to the needs of a young person, but he has to have also sufficient experience to enable him to produce realistic proposals for the teaching situation. Much of the developing methodology of the designer can be of great value in the organization of teaching material, and experience of design is important for the teacher in this respect as well as for its direct role in children's education.

The school situation – the education industry

As well as briefly summarizing significant changes in society and their effect on the work of the art teacher, it would be unrealistic not to relate the resulting educational needs to limitations and possibilities within the school situation. What follows is a generalized picture. Fortunately not all of the following difficulties are found in every school, but it is obvious from our own observations that most teachers are having to work under some of those discussed.

In a large proportion of schools it is a matter of fact that subjects based principally on practical work (like art and handicraft) have not, for a long time, been held in such high esteem as more academic studies. The reasons for this comparatively low status are complex and are partially related to traditional class barriers in society. We shall be considering the problem of lack of status later – here we shall simply look at the limitations this imposes.

Time

One of the fundamental problems is that the child in the secondary school does not spend as much time in the art room as in some others. The limited time factor may take many forms. In some schools lower age groups may experience little art education; in others early option schemes deprive many older children of any opportunity to pursue art studies to any depth. An even more cynical view of the value of art education is found where it is used to provide a little light relief from the pressures of advanced studies for the sixth form.

Class size

Closely linked with the problem of time is the size of art classes. Although the situation is improving, there is still quite wide disparity from school to school and area to area, where teaching groups may range from four to forty! For those involved in the teaching of a subject which is essentially practical, this situation can be physically and mentally exhausting and is inclined to lessen the urge to experiment and innovate.

Space

Class size leads on naturally to the question of space and facilities. Luckily it may only be in a minority of schools that the feeling still exists that art education is not useful enough to warrant specialist rooms. Many art rooms are still equipped, however, like Victorian classrooms and facilities for research and experiment are limited. While much thought is now being given to the re-designing of space and facilities, the responsibility for getting the best out of the present situation lies with the individual teacher. The basic problem is really one of organization. Even a small amount of time spent in investigating the working situation and reorganizing the facilities and equipment to meet demands more efficiently can improve the most apparently intractable situation.

Money

The lack of facilities, equipment and materials reflects the fact that generally too little money is available. While this situation exists, it again requires a great deal of ingenuity and organizing power on the part of the teacher if he is to extend the work beyond the traditional limits imposed by paint and paper. Too little effort is being spent on discovering sources of supply that are more efficient and less expensive. Traditional sources may not always provide the most appropriate solutions to this problem.

   The local art advisory staff can help the teacher in many ways to overcome some of these practical difficulties. Solutions to the problem of organizing resources can also come from studying the ways in which industry itself overcomes these problems which involve economy and efficiency.

Examinations

Some teachers claim that the system of examinations is a very limiting factor preventing the introduction of new educational concepts. As described elsewhere in this book (page 27) attempts are being made to create GCE (General Certificate of Education) syllabuses which are liberal enough to encompass the generous growth of dynamic educational ideas. Developments in connexion with the CSE (Certificate of Secondary Education) have already gone a long way towards indicating the possibilities for a more realistic examination system. Most creative teachers have found it possible to develop courses which are broad in approach and allow the children to take formal examinations in their stride.

33

Curriculum organization

The final aspect under discussion in this section is the relationship of art education to the other subjects in the school curriculum. Through isolation the art teacher may have to waste time, materials and effort in constructing experiences for the child which would more efficiently be carried out with inter-departmental co-operation. Pooled resources in terms both of facilities and specialist teaching experience would help greatly in the designing of broad-based educational programmes. In addition, the young person would be able to see more immediately the interrelationship between his various studies, and also their relevance to life in the adult world outside school.

Until comparatively recently, over-specialization in individual subjects has been proceeding at a great pace, and this has led to the links between them becoming strained and obscured. Now the speed of extreme specialization seems to have slowed a little, and the need for a fully integrated education is becoming more clearly understood. This means that broad areas of common ground between subjects can be recognized and explored more easily.

It is not the intention here to discuss all aspects of the role that the art teacher could play in inter-disciplinary education. It is difficult to find a group of subjects in the school curriculum where some form of co-operation has not been or could not be valuable in terms of interrelated educational experience.

To present all these possibilities is not within the terms of reference for this contribution, but as noted elsewhere in the book, three subjects exist where closer links are particularly appropriate to the educational concepts we are discussing. Science, handicraft, and art education have a firm foundation for co-operation in that fundamentally a large proportion of the activity is of a practical nature. The growth of inter-dependence in the existing school situation is taking place in three overlapping stages:

1 Physical isolation – departments in different parts of the school building
  Theoretical isolation – teaching programmes unco-ordinated

2 Physical isolation, but
  Preliminary theoretical links – development of co-operative projects

3 Physical proximity – new school building programmes, reorganization and/or additions to existing schools
  Total theoretical inter-dependence – co-ordinated teaching programmes determined by a single set of basic principles

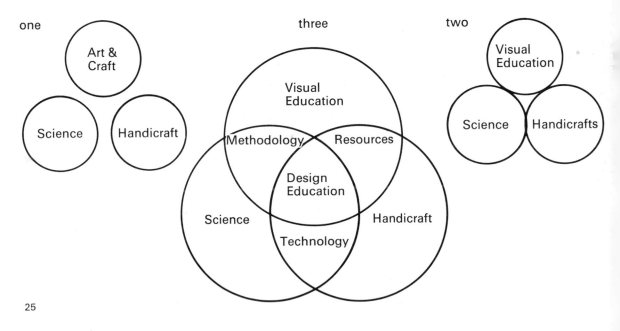

It is worth noting that the change in the character of activities in the art room from inward-looking to outward-looking concepts has made necessary a change in title from art to visual education. Although this title itself does not indicate the full range of perceptual activities involved, it will be used for the purposes of this contribution to indicate the re-orientation of art education in terms of a broader approach based on the needs of the individual in an urban industrial society.

The desire and need for growing inter-departmental co-operation throw fresh responsibilities on the art teacher. It makes necessary in the first instance a reappraisal of the content of teaching programmes, and secondly the development of the ability to communicate in non-specialist language the aims and content of visual education. The art teacher who does not wish to remain in isolation will have to make an effort to understand the aims and problems of teaching other specialist subjects.

This preliminary argument has been an attempt to define in very general terms some of the problems and developments in the school situation which will affect the efforts of the art teacher to organize more realistic teaching programmes. It can be seen that these problems are largely organizational ones involving the co-ordination of content and facilities. They are the kind of limitations that many designers have to face in solving complex problems, and it is from the systematic methods that designers use that the art teacher can gain valuable information and planning experience.

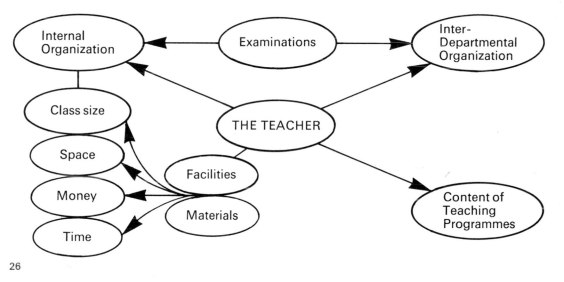

26

Development of teaching programmes – the educational product

So far we have considered in general terms the changes in our society which have presented the specialist art teacher with a major educational problem. We turn now to the main aim which is to indicate some of the work which is going on in the development of relevant teaching programmes for the present art-room situation.

We are only just beginning to see what are the practical educational implications of industrial society. There is much to discover and the ideas put forward here are not intended to be a stock of ready-made solutions to be transplanted into every teaching situation. Teaching programmes will of course always have to be developed in accordance with the circumstances of the particular teacher, child and school. We hope that these examples and the way in which they were developed may act as an indication of the richer potential left as yet unexplored.

Perhaps two points need to be made clear from the outset. First, in considering the mass of objects and organizations which constitute the designed environment, we are not in any way concerned with propagating 'good taste'. There is no question of trying to impose a single set of aesthetic values on the young person. We are not involved in any process which results in showering the child with examples of design that have been classified as good or bad by an external body. The aim is rather to defend and encourage the individual's freedom of choice and criticism based on a reasoned understanding.

Secondly, we are not convinced of any real educational value in nebulous forms of design appreciation in schools. This has tended to set the designer apart, surrounding him by as much mystique as the artist. The dangers of this approach are that the study tends to be largely passive and to revolve round currently 'with-it' styles. Uninformed judgement tends eventually to rely on the opinions of others and to place too much emphasis on stylistically fashionable commodities. Examples used in this kind of approach are too often those which tend to suggest that the child's tastes should coincide with those of the Sunday colour supplements – an unrealistic proposal, even if it could be shown to be desirable.

One of the most dynamic qualities of visual education is that it is based on a practical experience of investigation and expression. This principle forms the foundation for all the examples shown here. In this context, the major problem becomes one of evolving logical programmes of practical educational experience that will make it possible for the individual to develop his or her understanding. This understanding will grow most strongly from a familiarity with the reasons behind the visual, emotional and functional realities of designed products.

The question this raises immediately is how do we identify and give priority to those aspects of the environment and social pressures around us which it is necessary to understand? One way to create some order out of the confusion is to attempt to classify the fluid situation into a form where these aspects become clearer. Any such classification will inevitably be generalized, but it will present the possibility for a logical framework upon which to base our approach. One such approach that seems appropriate is to determine the cycle of events that gives rise to the man-made objects in the everyday world.

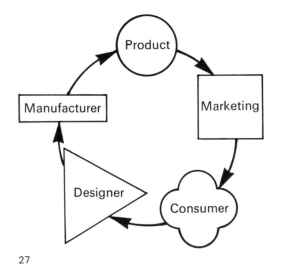

27

This applies to all objects in the environment, large or small – soap-powders or architecture. The cycle as drawn is very much an over-simplification. For example, if the designer always produced solutions which perfectly met the needs of the consumer it would be possible to argue that there would be no educational problem at all. However, as Peter Goldman shows, this is far from being the case. Marketing and advertising are creating wants to be satisfied, so that the designer cannot refer directly to needs as expressed by the consumer. Also, the cycle is not a continuous movement in one direction. The diagram demonstrates that for the young person to develop an understanding of the reasons behind the psychological and utilitarian function of products it is necessary to investigate the role of the designer, the manufacturer, the marketing manager and the consumer.

Designer

A designer can be defined simply as a person who solves problems. Problem-solving is a basic human activity in which we are all engaged – the designer extends the potential of problem-solving by adopting a methodical approach. Problem-solving plays a predominant role in the activities and educational experiences which we are discussing. It is a rational, decision-making process, and in some aspects differs radically from many traditional forms of art and craft education which have been more concerned with irrational, intuitive experiences. This is not to argue that subjective, intuitive work should cease, but that the concept of visual education should be broadened to include both subjective *and* objective practical experiences. It is difficult to see how *reasoned* understanding can develop from purely *intuitive* activities. There are many young people who feel that the art lesson is invalid for them because they 'can't draw' or 'can't paint'. A problem-solving approach makes the chances of their involvement greater as it need not rely upon any narrow craft or skill for its development.

Problem-solving can be used as the vehicle for an immediate experience – for example, where manipulation of a material provides a direct solution. At the other extreme it can provide the basis for a prolonged project involving much preliminary research and organization of information. This range of experience in its extended and immediate forms is seen as the basic essence of the intended art-room activity. Diagram 28 shows the framework of a systematic approach to problem-solving as used by designers of many kinds.

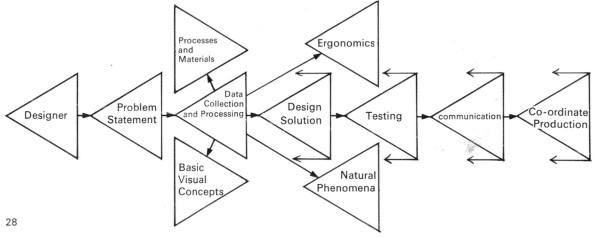

28

The initial problem or instruction given to the designer is usually in a garbled form which he has to sort out and re-define in exact terms. Complex problems may have to be broken down into many smaller components and each solved with regard to their effect on one another.

It is as well to bear in mind that for lower age groups especially a teacher must define very clearly any problem which is given to a class. An example of a mis-statement occurred recently when a teacher set a problem using drinking-straws, intending that groups of second-year children should gain experience of the structural principle of how a small amount of material can support a relatively large weight. Unfortunately the problem was posed as 'support this brick with a structure in straws'; the result: four boxes of straws in a heap, over which was poured a large quantity of adhesive. In other words the range of intended limitations had not been fully expressed in the problem.

Problem
Statement

This fundamental difficulty which we all experience when attempting precisely to define our problems can be demonstrated by a simple questioning technique. For example, we could describe a deceptively simple situation such as 'sitting at the table, in a crowded restaurant, my cup of tea is suddenly upset – what is my problem?'. The typical answers given to this problem soon show that we have become accustomed to providing solutions that may or may not be apt, rather than to stating the problem precisely. As a result, we tend to think that the problem is 'to change your trousers quickly' or 'to mop up the tea' or 'to order another tea' and so on, whereas these are, in fact, all partial solutions to a problem not expressed. This kind of discussion can be effective as a form of mental limbering up for a period of practical problem-solving activity.

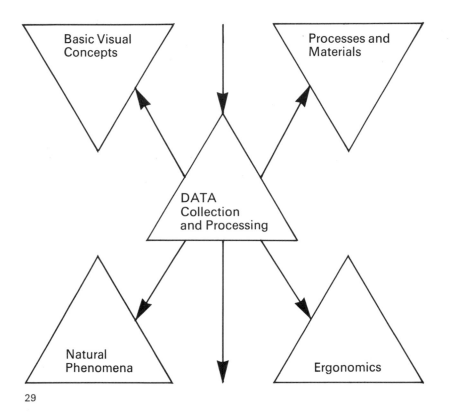

29

Having defined the problem, the designer has then to set about collecting information and organizing it in such a way that it will help him create an efficient solution. The amount and type of data he requires will depend upon the nature and magnitude of the problem he has to solve. Designers normally possess a certain amount of information on their particular area of activity based on previous experience and training. However, the current speed of change in technological developments and rapid alterations in the pattern of complex human needs have made it more and more necessary that the designer becomes part of a team where he acts as co-ordinator in the collection and analysis of essential information. I have selected for inclusion in the diagram only four examples which seem to be particularly relevant to the art-room activities we are examining.

Data collection and processing are fundamental pursuits natural to many young people. Stamp collecting and scrap albums are two examples where an amorphous mass of material is systematically organized. This desire to obtain and organise information should be encouraged – magazines and newspapers provide ample visual material on a broad spectrum of industrial society.

A study of basic visual concepts includes a large proportion of the work at present playing a predominant part in visual education. It deals in general terms with all the purely visual concepts that relate to the appearance of designed products – line, tone, colour, mass, space, form, rhythm, pattern, etc. Because it provides a basic visual vocabulary necessary for the examination of more complex concepts, this study ideally comes at the earliest stage in a teaching programme. This section includes the investigation of the ways in which we perceive our environment.

The illustrations opposite show simple devices, constructed by third-year boys, to test aspects of illusion and ambiguity of single-eye vision. In this way many of the factors involved in the theory of perception can be studied in a practical way.

38

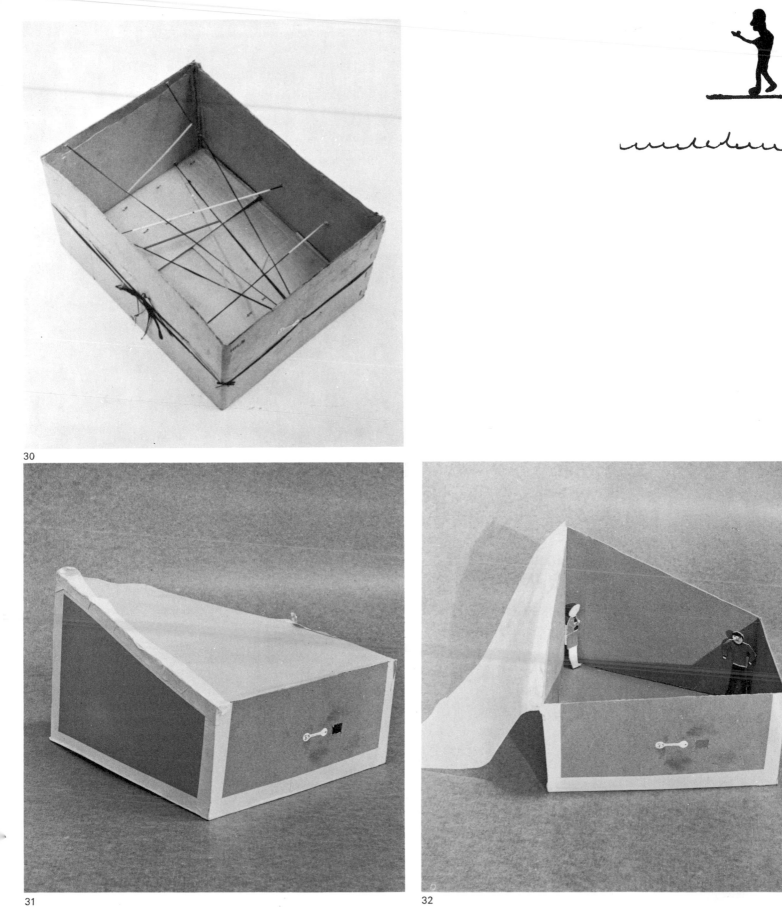

It is not proposed to deal in any detail with this area of work, as many valuable visual-education activities have already become fundamental and familiar to the art room. The aim is to concentrate instead on those aspects which may be less well known.

Processes and Materials

A basic experience of the wide variety of materials and processes utilized in the production of man-made objects is another essential aspect of the early stages of the teaching programme. It seems important that the nature of this experience should be one which allows the discovery of the widest possible potential of material or process, unhampered by craft traditions or skill barriers.

Man is rapidly discovering many forms of new materials and inventing new forms of technology to exploit them. If the activity in the art room is solely concerned with paint and paper or the tradi-

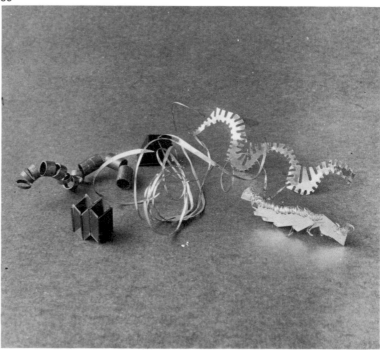

tional materials of the sculptor – clay, plaster, stone – this will tend to increase the child's impression that experience in the art room is unreal and unrelated to the world outside school (figs. 33–5).

36

Many of the materials in daily use by industry may be too costly to be extensively employed in the art room at the present time, but there is an unlimited and largely untapped source of material in the form of commercial and industrial waste (fig.36). Many types of such material have a basic educational potential inherent in themselves – the act of handling a punched out metal strip, for example, starts the child thinking about the repetitive, mechanized process that gave rise to its form. The manipulation of such material induces a creative, problem-solving situation in that there are no traditional ways of working for the child to refer to or to be hindered by.

The growth of do-it-yourself activities in the home has increased the child's familiarity with hand-held tools and his awareness of any hazards to safety. With a little organization this kind of equipment can be brought into the art room to extend the range of available processes so that they relate more directly to those used in industry.

Equipment for working with newer materials can be costly – particularly plastics – but many expensive processes can be analysed and much cheaper versions produced. The examples (figs. 37–8)

37   38

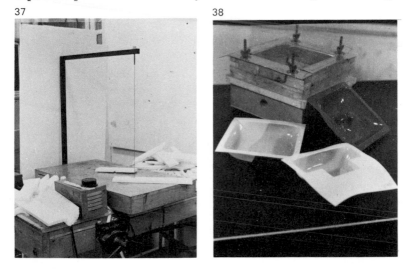

are a hot-wire cutter for expanded polystyrene and a vacuum-forming machine that have been made very cheaply and used in the art room.

I have deliberately placed the emphasis on increasing the range of processes and materials for three-dimensional work, since at the present time art-room activity still consists largely of two-dimensional experience, while we live in an environment which is mainly three dimensional.

However, there is also a need to increase the range of two-dimensional image-making processes, particularly those related to repetitive industrial procedures like printing, rather than the production of unique, one-off items like paintings.

39   40   41

A third area of expansion for art-room facilities is related to other forms of mass media – photography, film and television. Many schools now possess film-making and projection equipment, tape recorders, concept projectors, still cameras and even closed-circuit television. Much of this equipment is only used at fairly infrequent intervals for specialist reasons – to record the school play or the annual school trip, or only as visual aids. It is time that they were fully utilized in the art room as a part of visual education. In this situation they could provide invaluable practical visual experience related directly to the young person's own surroundings, as in the photographs shown above.

The study of natural form has long been a part of visual education. It is a rich source of imagery and pattern, and provides a vehicle on which to base graphic skills. A deeper analytical approach to understanding the structure behind natural form and the system behind the structure reveals the source of many design ideas used in the man-made environment. By working in this way the young

42

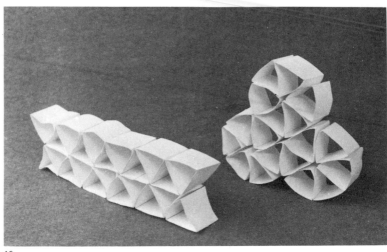

43

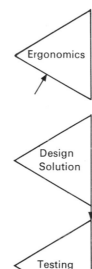

person is able to draw upon his experiences in the science laboratory and relate them to those that take place in the art room (figs. 42–3).

One example of this is the relationship between cellular aggregates and man's use of standardized unit components. Here the child brings together constructional and visual experience and explores a fundamental relationship between science and vision in the development of the man-made world.

Ergonomics is an important aspect of the designer's activity which makes it possible for him to produce more efficient solutions. Ergonomics has been defined in many ways, but it is simply the collection of information which will help towards the production of a designed object that can be used efficiently by a human being. An obvious example of this is the test rig used in the furniture industry in order to determine the criteria for more comfortable seats. An experience of this kind of data-collecting is important for an understanding of design, but it is also a way of studying the whole question of man's physiological capacity.

The designer, having produced a solution based on the data which he has collected, must then find ways of ensuring that it meets as far as possible all the requirements he has defined in the original problem.

In the teaching situation problem-solving without the opportunity to test the solutions is educationally invalid. It is in testing his solutions that the child is able to see how well he has understood the problem and how efficient his thinking is in relation to others. In the same way the teacher is able to assess how clearly he has set the problem, and to judge the development of understanding in the young person.

The testing of designed objects which are solutions to specific problems can lead to much collective discussion in which the experience of individuals is shared. This talking stage can be of great help to those children with less intellectual ability because it does not centre around nebulous phrases, such as 'I like it', or 'I don't like it', or 'it is interesting'. Instead, this type of discussion has its foundation in the different methods of approach adopted, which are in evidence in the form of tangible practical solutions giving rise to rational argument. In this way the child increases his understanding through an experience of alternative methods, which he may then be able to apply in the next problem-solving situation.

Later on we shall examine more closely methods of testing solutions in connexion with particular aspects of the man-made environment, but the responsibilities of the designer do not end here. The process of developing a finally satisfactory design is not linear, but is composed of many cycles where information is fed back from tests and experience. The problem may have to be re-defined, more data collected and the solution modified. But in the end the designer is faced with the task of communicating the solution to those who are responsible for its manufacture; he also has to follow its production through to ensure that the effectiveness of the design is in no way reduced by sloppy production control.

It is not possible to go into greater detail about the role of the designer and the design process within the terms of reference of this book. It is hoped, however, that the few aspects which have been examined are sufficient to demonstrate its relevance to the art-room situation and its central position in the study of those aspects of the industrial, urban society which are included in the following sections.

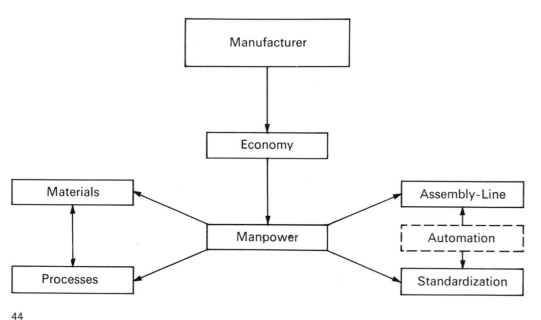

44

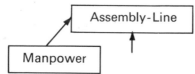

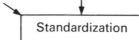

The increased utilization of industrial materials and processes in the classroom only relates to one particular aspect of industrial society. Diagram 44 shows some of the other sections of industrial activity which influence the visual and functional efficiency of man-made objects.

As we have said, most of the practical processes normally used in the art room involve the production of single, unique objects. These processes relate in manufacturing terms to those vanished days when a large part of the physical environment was produced by hand-craft methods. These items now form only a small and often expensive part of the mass of available goods. It is difficult to conceive any way in which a child can establish personal criteria of judgement of the mass-produced environment if all his practical experience is in terms of hand craftsmanship. It is important for the art teacher to provide the young person with experiences that help him to understand some of the problems of mass production. We shall next look briefly at ways of simulating three aspects of these problems in the art room.

Competitive group games can be used as one way of studying this feature of mass-production procedure. Industry itself is using similar methods in training its personnel.

The essential educational element is that each group is given the same simple problem to solve, involving several stages. They are asked to organize themselves efficiently to carry it out. Usually the length of time taken to reach a satisfactory conclusion is the major factor in assessing results. An important ingredient here is that the method of organization is documented, either after the process is completed or preferably during the activity itself. In this way details can be examined which may seem insignificant at the time, but which turn out to have played an important part in the process. The actual group game can be relatively commonplace, like assembling electric plugs or classifying an amorphous collection of objects according to size, colour, texture, etc.

When the game is complete, the relative merits of the systems used by each group can be discussed and extended further by extracting the most efficient aspects from the various solutions and combining them to produce an optimum solution.

These problems of systematic planning and the organization of manpower can form the basis for an understanding of assembly-line procedure.

The educational potential of organizational problems associated with group activity can be examined in conjunction with the investigation of standardization. One practical method is to examine a unit construction system where each member of the group is involved in the design and manufacture of a standard component. This type of problem can be posed in many ways – for example, as the production of a structure with twelve identical units, or a structure with no permanent joints, or a fully adaptable, demountable unit construction – rather like a child's constructional toy (figs. 45–6).

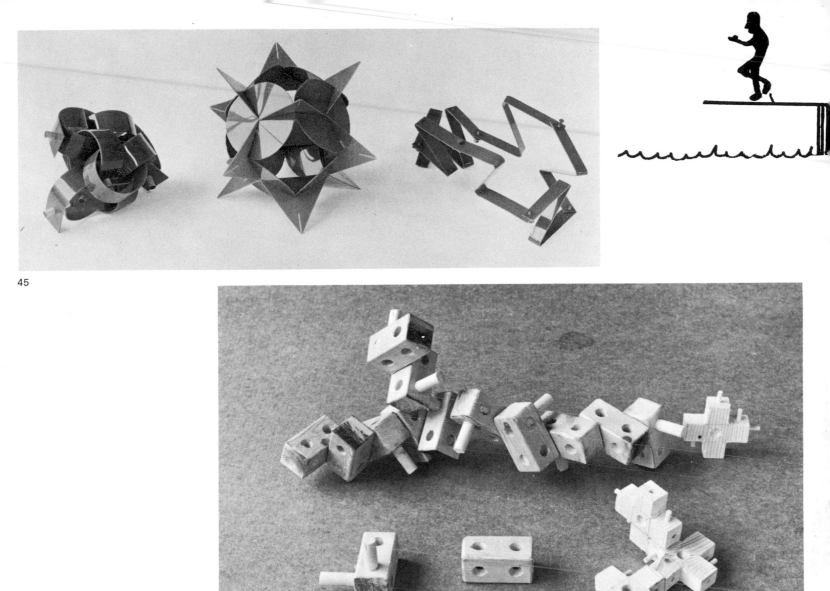

45

46

In addition to the problem of group organization the need for precision in measuring and working materials becomes apparent, especially when the individual components are assembled into a single structure. In this way the need for precision is built into the problem and not imposed artificially. The results are self-testing in that the individuals involved will discuss the efficiency of one another's attempts at the assembly stage. This kind of approach to standardization, unit construction and the value of precision could be of use in the art room or the handicraft workshop during an introductory study of materials and processes.

Another major manufacturing concept which greatly affects the appearance and function of objects in the industrial environment is the economical use of materials and processes. The problem of making a product economically without impairing its visual, emotional, or utilitarian efficiency is again an aspect which can play an important part in education. The implications for the financially impoverished art room should be encouraging. The concept can be extended through the use of all media. For example, in two dimensions the problem could be that of containing the maximum amount of visual information in a small area, to be legible at a specified distance. Economy is implicit in the formulation of the problem.

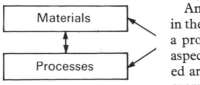

THE FUNCTIONAL ORGANISATION OF SPACE - (1) - AS A CONTAINER.

BRIEF

1. Construct a container which allows all the forms within to be seen from at least one external viewpoint.

2. Organise the space in the container to produce maximum restriction of movement of the forms inside.

3. Material: Card - use the least amount possible.

4. Processes: Cutting, bending, adhesives.
   (a) Keep processing to a minimum.
   (b) Avoid wastage of material as a result of processing.

5. Time Limit: 90 minutes.

Fill in the details below as accurately as possible:-

			unit grams
	Total initial weight of card taken from sheet		unit grams
(a)	Total weight of container empty		grams
(b)	Weight of wastage		grams
(c)	Number of cuts made		cuts
(d)	Total length of cuts made		inches
(e)	Number of bends made		bends
(f)	Total length of bent edges		inches
(g)	Area of adhesive used		sqr.inches
(h)	Displacement efficiency *		-
	TOTAL		-

* DISPLACEMENT EFFICIENCY
This will be assessed as follows:-

1. The container and contents will be dropped from height of 36 inches onto a hard surface.

2. A still camera will record any displacement that occurs as a result of impact.

3. A figure showing efficiency relative to others tested in this way will be arrived at from examination of the photographic record.

IMPORTANT: MARK CLEARLY ON THE CONTAINER, THE LETTER SHOWN IN THE TOP RIGHT HAND CORNER OF THIS PAGE.

47

Again, in the packaging brief illustrated above, the problem was to contain all the elements securely, using a minimum amount of card, adhesive and forming processes. The containers were tested by dropping them from a height of thirty-six inches. The data sheet was completed for each solution and amounts of materials were weighed and measured. The concluding discussion involved ideas about the effect of economy of material on the appearance of the packages.

While these aspects of logical thinking and controlled use of processes and materials are implicit in some of the present art-room experiences, they are probably more common to the mathematics, science, or handicraft departments. However, experience of the rational, decision-making processes of the designer and manufacturer is essential in leading to a reasoned understanding of industrial products.

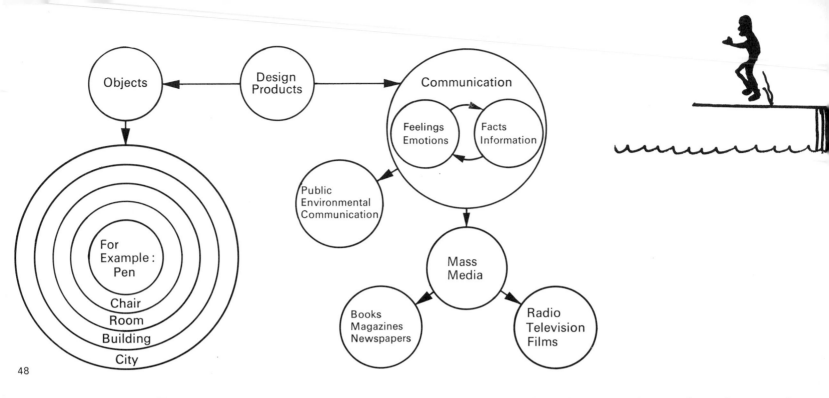

48

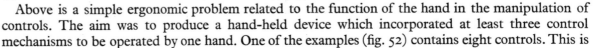

Design
Products

Out of the vast quantity and variety of designed products those shown here are just a few examples of work carried out by teachers, students and young people in secondary schools, and arranged in two very generalized categories as seen in diagram 48. Utilitarian design products have been classified as 'Objects'; where the product is the transmission of information or ideas, they have been classified as 'Communication'.

Many aspects covered in these two categories are interrelated and the classification is only intended to help in identifying where the *emphasis* of a particular study lies. For example, if we were examining the construction of a television set, this would be classified as the study of an object. If, on the other hand, we were examining the content of a television programme then this would be an aspect of communication. A significant interrelationship would occur if we were studying the social or emotional significance of the appearance of a television set – then we would again be concerned with the communicating potential of form, colour, texture, etc.

To give this section a sensible structure, objects in the environment are grouped together according to size. At the centre we find the small personal range of design products, while at the outside are cities and towns, with the intermediate stages falling in between.

The examples are not intended as how-to-do-it formulas for every teaching situation, but are shown here to demonstrate the nature of the problem-solving approach.

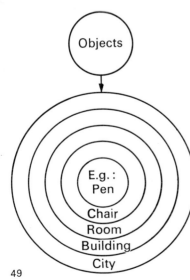

49

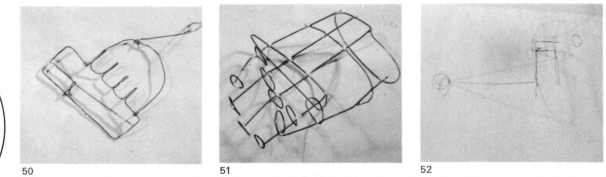

50   51   52

Above is a simple ergonomic problem related to the function of the hand in the manipulation of controls. The aim was to produce a hand-held device which incorporated at least three control mechanisms to be operated by one hand. One of the examples (fig. 52) contains eight controls. This is

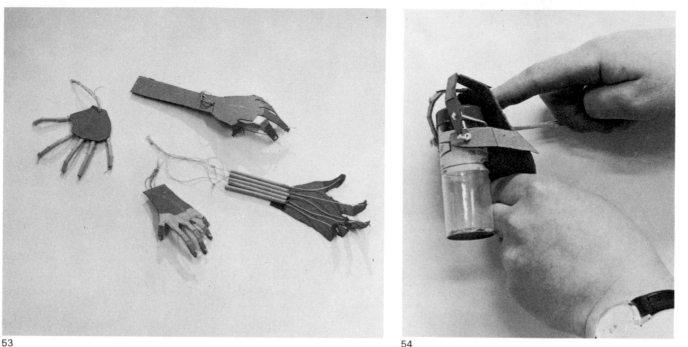

53

54

evidence of the way in which this kind of problem can lead to extremely creative extensions. A bi-product of this problem is the increased awareness of the exact nature of the human form – those who were involved stated that they had discovered more about the hand through solving this simple problem than in many hours of conventional drawing.

Illustrations 53–6 taken from a project with third-year children. Simple diagrams were used initially as a means of investigating and communicating the movements of the hand. The second stage of the problem was to use this information to design an articulated-hand construction, capable of gripping small objects. Only very basic materials such as cardboard, string and sticky brown paper were used in achieving quite sophisticated solutions.

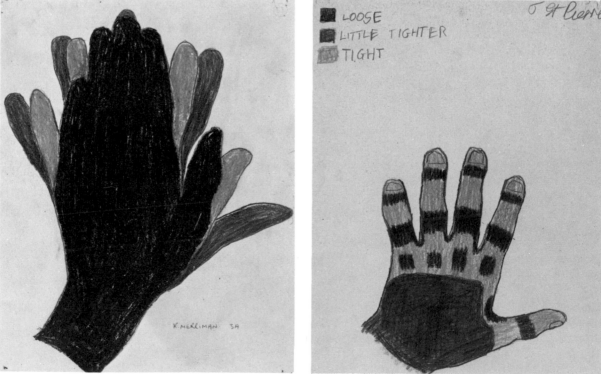

LOOSE
LITTLE TIGHTER
TIGHT

55

56

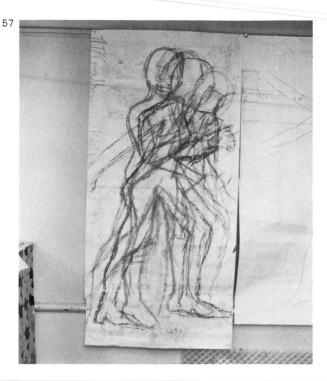
57

58

59

Another activity in which the collection of ergonomic information played an important part: a group of girls in their last year at school were asked to design a dress suitable to wear in a bowling alley. Studies of the movements involved in bowling were made first of all (fig. 57), and then prototype dresses were produced which were tested to reveal weaknesses. Signs of premature wear and tear were noted at the stress points and the dresses modified until an efficient solution was obtained. Through this practical experience with a specialist problem the girls became aware that there is more involved in fashion design than mere stylistic changes. Subsequent work involved the analysis of everyday clothing from the same standpoint.

49

60

61

Above are examples of structural activities which provide an experience basic to the understanding of the chair-designer's problems. By using unfamiliar material the students were forced to consider fresh structural possibilities. In both cases the structure was required to utilize a minimum amount of material to support the weight of a person at a specified distance from the floor.

62

63

Figs. 62–3 show an analytical approach to the study of the function of a folding chair. Measurements and other data for various seating positions formed another part of the programme. This approach emphasizes the use of drawing as a way of collecting and communicating precise information.

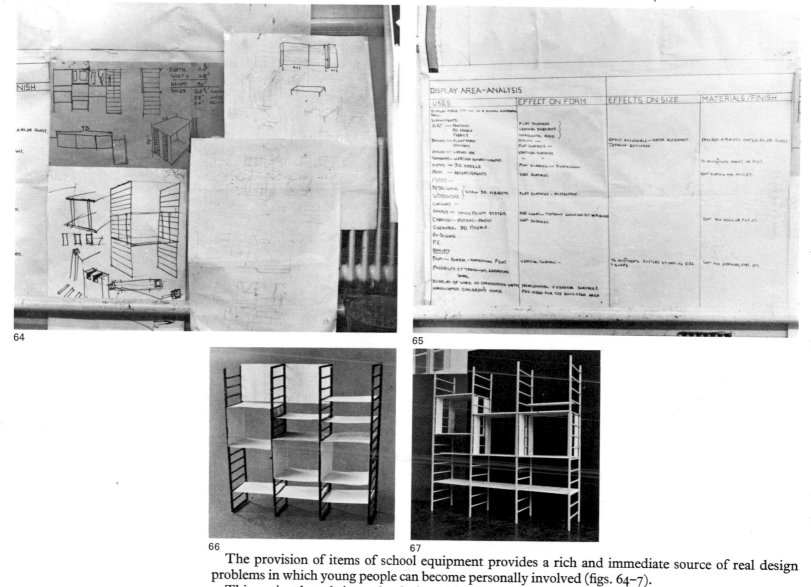

64

65

66

67

The provision of items of school equipment provides a rich and immediate source of real design problems in which young people can become personally involved (figs. 64–7).

This project lasted six weeks, during which the children were all taking part in detailed preliminary planning and in the collection of information on the function of a display system. The project, which was organized jointly by the art and handicraft departments, then extended to the manufacture of small-scale models and finally the production of the full-size product. In this problem-solving project the children experienced many aspects of the designer's problems and his methodology for solving them.

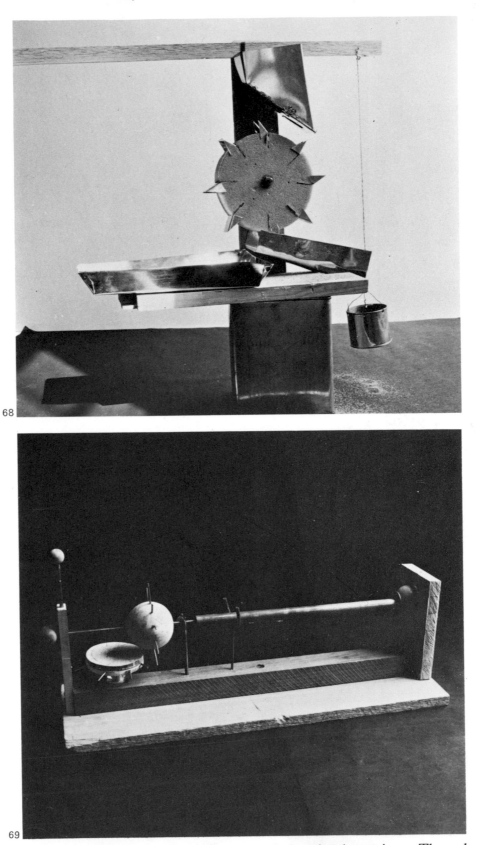

68

69

Simple machines provide a rich source of educational experience. Those shown here are examples of a basic problem in harnessing energy into a useful form. The sources of energy were commonplace – water flow, sand, rubber bands, etc. The materials were chosen so that they were relatively simple to

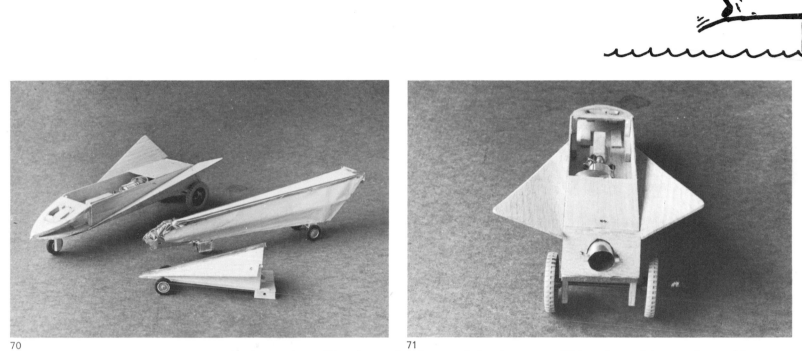

70   71

manipulate – sheet tin, soft wood and expanded polystyrene. Using these elements the problem was to produce rotation in one plane and transfer it to become rotation in another. The examples in illustrations 70–1 show work from a group of fourth-year boys. Out of their interest in machines grew the problem of harnessing the power of model jet engines in an attempt to predict the nature of vehicles in the future. The boys' existing experience of model-making and their active interest in the world of motor-bikes and cars provided the stimulus to maintain interest over a long period.

One aspect of the design of the interior of buildings and rooms is spatial organization. Illustrations 72–3 show examples of young people manipulating lightweight panels using a systematic method that was coherent visually and capable of controlling the movement of people. Experience

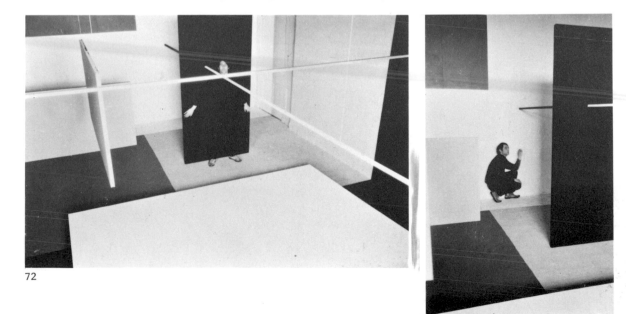

72

73

with the visual and physical problems of interior organization can lead on to the analysis of specific interiors. Designing the set for the school play can also provide a similar experience if the children are involved at all levels and not just used to slap on the paint. This kind of activity provides a basis for an analysis of familiar interiors such as the art room itself – even leading on to its re-design. Similar criteria can then be applied to the home environment.

These are attempts by secondary-school children to suggest possibilities for improving their home environments based on practical experience gained in the art room. Direct experience of the visual and physical aspects of room interiors enables the young person to create his own personalized environment based on logical reasoning as well as on tastes and preferences.

74

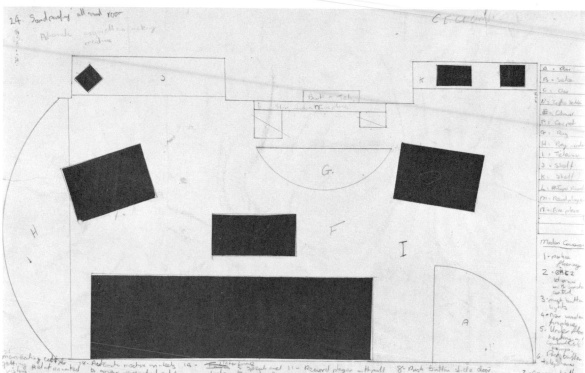

24. Sandpaper all over room

Provide acoustic packing
medium

A - Door
B - Sofa
C - Door
D - Coffee Table
E - Chair
F - Carpet
G - Rug
H - Bay window
I - Television
J - Shelf
K - Shelf
L - Tape Record
M - Record player
N - Fire place

Modern Conveniences

1 - parquet flooring
2 - One volume in the speaker control
3 - push button lights
4 - Mock wooden fireplace
5 - Under floor heating in concrete
6 - Push button telephone
7 - Conveyor belt (round room level floors)
8 - Push button slide door
9 - Push button (slide out cupboard) sliding doors
10 - Double glaze windows

75

76

One of the basic structural problems encountered in architecture is that of achieving an efficient vertical construction using the minimum amount of materials. This problem was simulated in the art room using lightweight materials such as balsa wood, paper and card. Simple methods of validating the solutions were adopted. Domestic scales were used to record the maximum load before breaking point. Still-photography and cinefilm were essential ways of studying these structures under load, as many of them were tested to destruction. Slides and films provided the material for discussion and evaluation after testing.

77

78

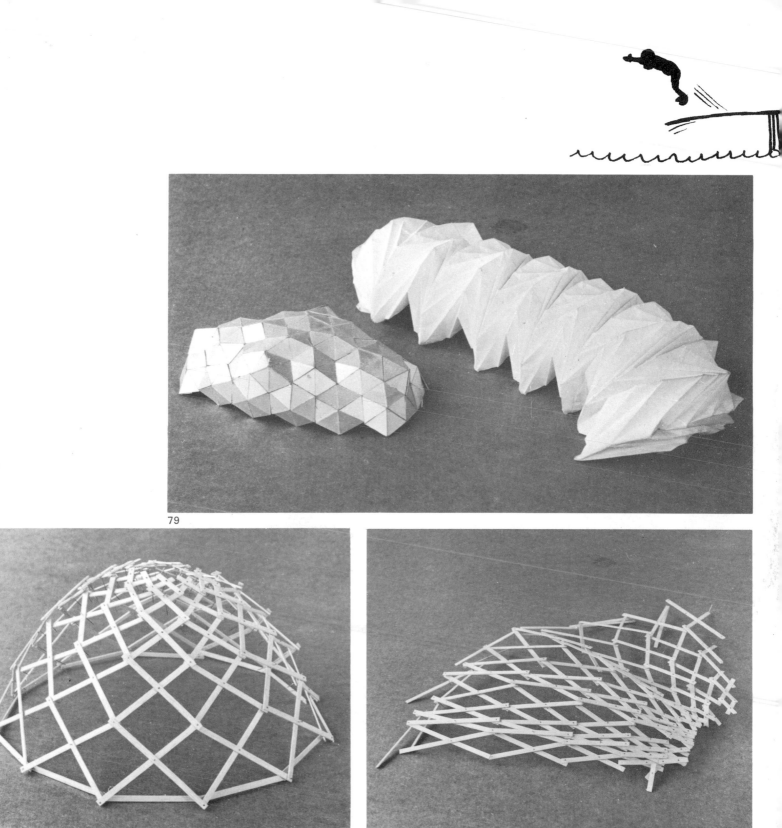

79

80   81

Another aspect of architecture which can be experienced in the art room is that of enclosing a volume of space efficiently. Shown here are permanent and demountable structures which offer solutions to these problems. Again the activity involved economical exploitation of the materials which were relatively simple to manipulate.

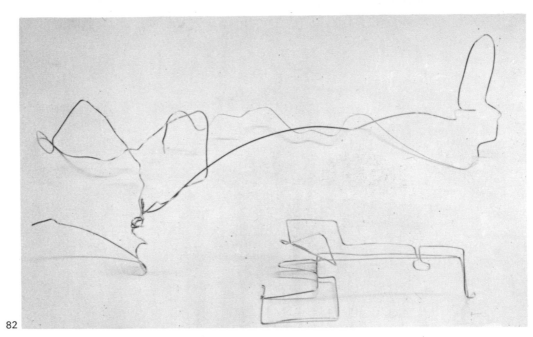

82

Above are three-dimensional 'drawings' made while walking around two floors of a school building. Soft wire was chosen for its ease of manipulation. This is just one method by which people can begin to be aware of the way in which buildings determine movement and activity.

It is possible to evolve work for the art room which simulates design for large-scale civil engineering. The examples below relate to bridge-building and space-spanning situations. In the first instance a general problem was set of spanning the greatest possible space using the minimum amount of

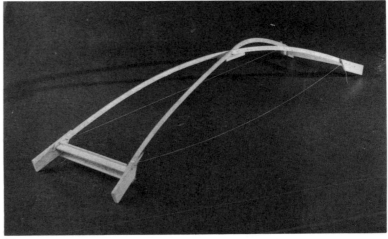

84

83

85

material. Then specific concepts were explored – the cantilever principle is shown above. The educational potential of all these activities is greatly increased where they are followed up by visits and the collection of further documentary evidence.

86

87

Illustrations 86–9 record examples from a group project lasting several weeks, undertaken by girls of 14 to 16. The aim was to study the way in which the form of the environment influences the movement of people within it.

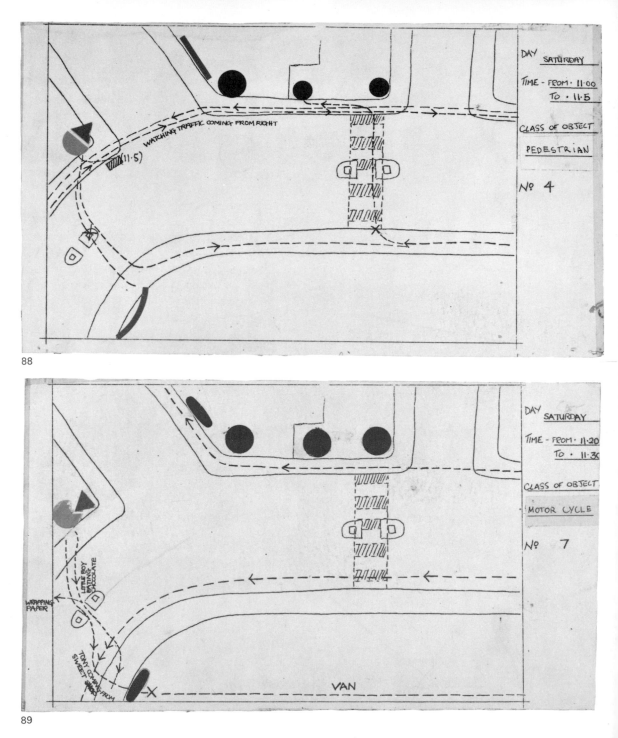

The activity began with experiments involving the control of inanimate objects – first a sphere in a two-dimensional maze, then a curtain ring on a complex three-dimensional structure. This was followed by the design of an adaptable environment for a mouse which made it possible to study the effects of form upon the freely chosen movements of a small animal.

For the final stage a busy road junction was selected. Using charts, diagrams, tape-recorded commentary, still-photography and cinefilm an extensive study of the physical factors of town planning (or the lack of it) was carried out for a small typical section of the environment.

In this tightly programmed project each stage provided the experience necessary to make logical decisions about the next and as a by-product a great deal of insight into techniques of observation and data collection was gained.

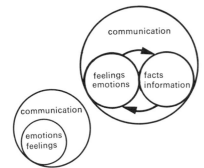

The next set of examples is that concerned with mass communication as a product of an industrial society. There are two distinct aspects here, involving the communication of feeling and emotions and the precise communication of facts and information.

These bottle forms are solutions to a communication problem. A selection of advertisements for cosmetics for men and women was supplied as a source of information upon which to base the forms. The brief was to assess the intentions of the advertiser and then to create a bottle form which communicated the same feelings. All evidence of the actual container forms was removed from the advertisements beforehand so that preconceptions were avoided. As well as the male and female qualities, a third problem was suggested which involved the production of bottle forms, to contain poison, which were repellent to children (fig. 92).

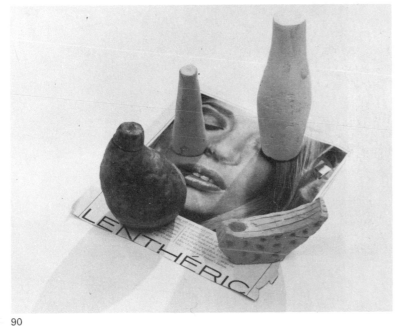

90

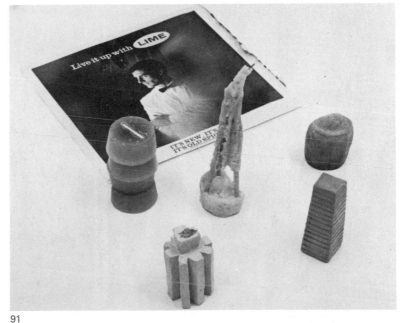

91

92

93

94

DISORDER

95

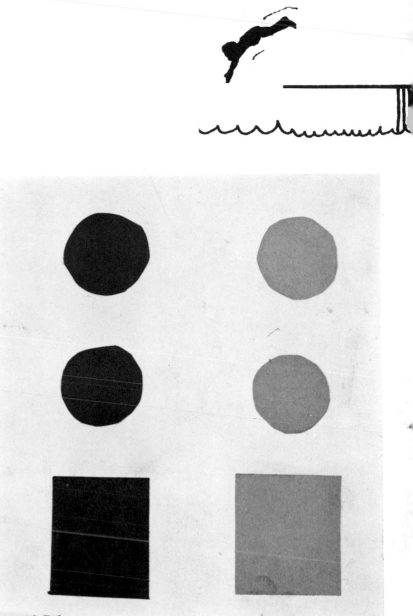

ORDER

96

The basic graphic processes of painting and drawing were employed in this exercise as the media for the communication of specific feelings and emotions. The letter-forms resulted from an analysis of the way in which lettering is used emotively in magazine advertisements. The actual shapes come from these 14-year-olds' attempts to express particular sensations and are not the result of tasteful preferences (figs. 93–4).

Cut-out geometrical paper shapes provided the means for similar investigation of the communicating power of basic elements, in monochrome, for a group of 13-year-olds. Here the problem was to communicate in a more symbolic way without using the written word (figs. 95–6).

Since psychology is a relatively new science, we as yet know little about the control and measurement of human response to this kind of visual communication. Hence a problem of this kind tends to be evaluated in fairly subjective terms. Nevertheless it is important to be aware that many forms of commercial products and mass communication utilize psychological factors which can influence our choice without our being aware of the pressures.

In contrast, when we are dealing with the communication of precise facts or information the validation of solutions becomes a much simpler and more rational process.

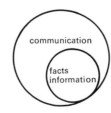

63

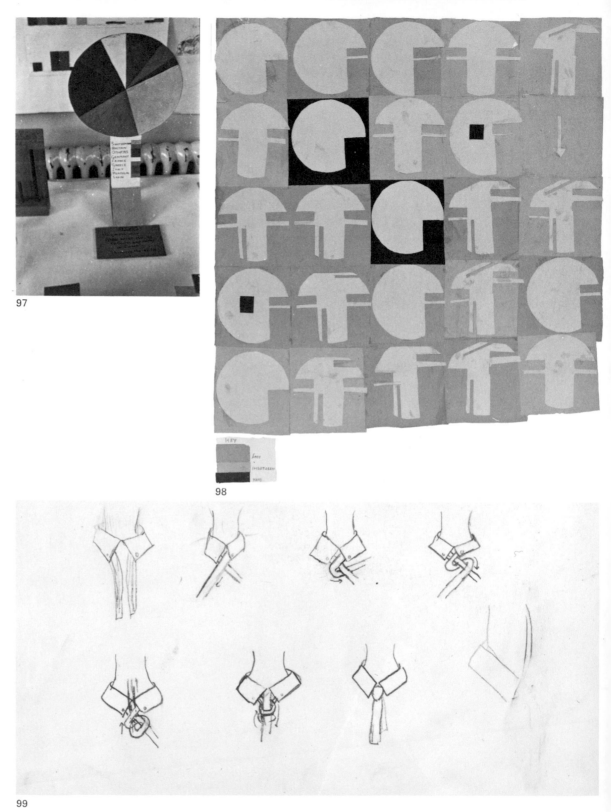

97

98

99

The first problem illustrated (fig.97) initially involved the collection of various items of information about preference for places for a European holiday. The children analysed the data and then attempted to communicate the content of the statistics in the form of a three-dimensional construction. The solutions were tested by checking whether communication actually took place. The second illustration (fig.98) shows an attempt by a 15-year-old to include two sets of information in one piece of visual

communication. The class time-table was analysed and a check made of the time spent per subject and individual preference for particular lessons. The problem was then to communicate this information using as little verbal material as possible.

The third example (fig.99) is of another problem which places the emphasis on visual forms of communication which do not rely upon words. Here the initial information does not consist of statistics, but is in the form of a precise sequence of events leading to the efficient completion of a particular operation. Again the first steps were to analyse the process, sort it out into its most logical stages and then select images and symbols which would communicate the operation.

The examples below and on the following page are taken from an extended game-making project. The design of simple games involves many aspects of visual communication and provides an emphasis

Starting with a square top left try to work round it in a kind of "diagonal symmetry"

1—26   Total output by 17.11.87

100

101

102

103

104

105

106

66

towards logical thinking, as well as collective planning and organization. The problem was to devise games for two or more players which depended on juxtaposition of colour and shape. The illustrations show initial work on ideas communicated through drawings, development of components, design, communication and construction of package. Final stages, also shown, included an investigation into efficient means for communicating the rules of the game and the contents of the package. The final illustration shows another solution to a similar problem.

Public Environmental Communication

Next comes an area of mass communication which is closely linked with town-planning. It covers all the vast proliferation of signs and symbols intended to give information and to instruct pedestrians and road-users. Before a child or adult can begin to evaluate the efficiency of this important aspect of urban life, it is necessary to have direct experience of the problems involved.

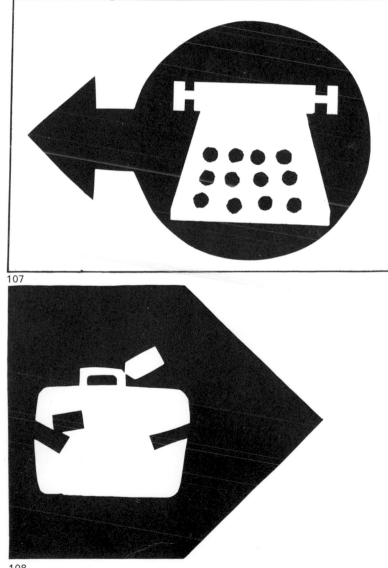

107

108

109

The school itself provides an opportunity for setting communication problems that can be tested in a real situation. Signs which give information on the nature of the activity which takes place in individual classrooms and direction-indicating diagrams for strategic locations in corridors are two examples. Problems which are abstracted directly from the external environment need to be made as realistic as possible by stating all the limitations in the problem, or better still by encouraging the children to draw up a list of the fundamental requirements themselves. In the signs shown on the previous page the distinction was carefully made between an image in a book and one which has to communicate at a considerable distance, say to a driver in a moving vehicle.

The airport sign was designed to be understood by a person moving at walking pace. In general the more factors that can be added to the definition of a problem like this, the more the sense of reality that can be achieved. It is through a sense of the real purpose behind mass communication that individuals can begin to build up a critical understanding of its effectiveness.

The amount of material in books, magazines and newspapers offers wide possibilities for developing relevant practical experiences.

Illustration 110 is an extension of the idea of the process diagram shown on page 64 where words are reduced to a minimum. In this case, however, the image was more closely related to the page format and the girls involved were given the opportunity to use their practical experience with paint and colour to increase the illustrative content. The map and the graph are two common examples where complex information is converted into a more easily assimilated visual form (figs. 111–2).

Books
Magazines
Newspapers

110

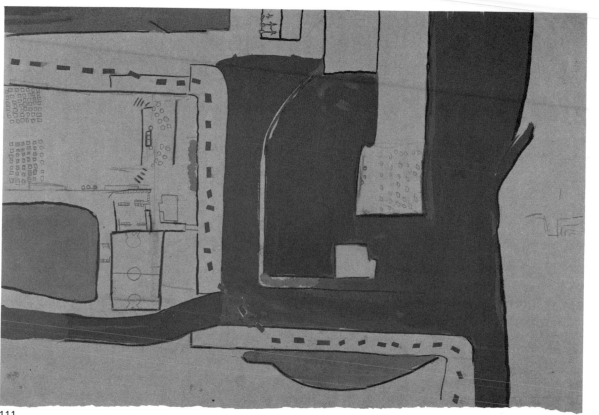

111

112

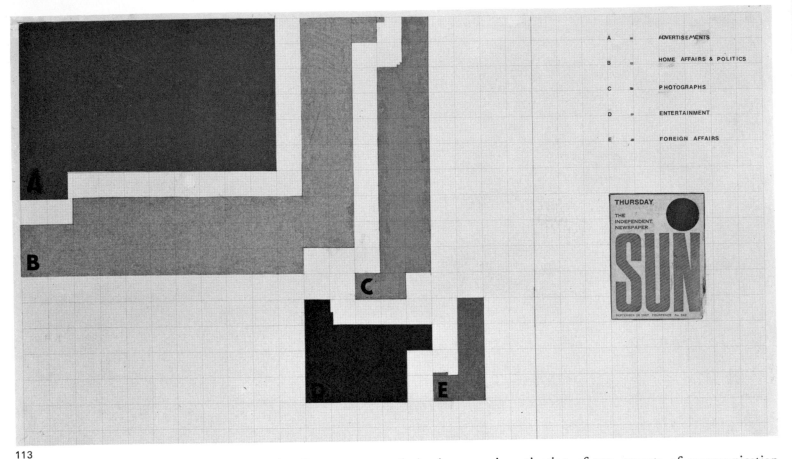

A = ADVERTISEMENTS

B = HOME AFFAIRS & POLITICS

C = PHOTOGRAPHS

D = ENTERTAINMENT

E = FOREIGN AFFAIRS

THURSDAY
THE
INDEPENDENT
NEWSPAPER
SUN

113

Radio
TV
Films

The example of newspaper analysis shows an investigation of two aspects of communication through this medium. In the first place the problem was to assess the content in terms of that most commonly read, and then work out percentage column space allocated to different topics. The final stage was the visual communication of the collected data.

School magazines provide an excellent vehicle for experiencing communication problems in a real situation. It is important that the young people should be involved at all stages in preparation and production, and not just considered as contributors of content. Many schools have now adopted, with encouraging results, this method of involving the children in a real design problem.

Television and the cinema are playing an increasingly important part in providing sources of vision for the young person. It is becoming urgent that we give at secondary-school level an experience that will help to develop an understanding of these two massive communication industries. It may be that the immediate reaction to providing this area of experience is that it is all too costly in terms of equipment and materials. There are possibilities, however, for introducing some of the fundamental aspects of these forms of communication without spending any extra money at all.

An experience of the continuity problems associated with the development of a sequence of inter-related events or storyline can be carried out using the traditional media of painting, drawing, collage, etc. Ideally the class as a whole determines the sequence through discussion and decides where the relevant sections of visual imagery are needed. The production of individual images can then be allocated to separate members of the class.

Many children possess their own cameras and still-photography can be used to produce the illustrations for the story-line. These images are usually clearly associated with those experienced on film and television. Sequences can be used to make particular observations of people or places. The potential experience with the storyline concept can be added to by using improvised dramatic situations as well (figs. 114–5).

The next illustrations show three stages in the development of a simple approach to the moving image. Using very inexpensive materials, devices like the flip-book can be made to gain experience in producing and controlling simple forms of animation. An example of flip animation is shown

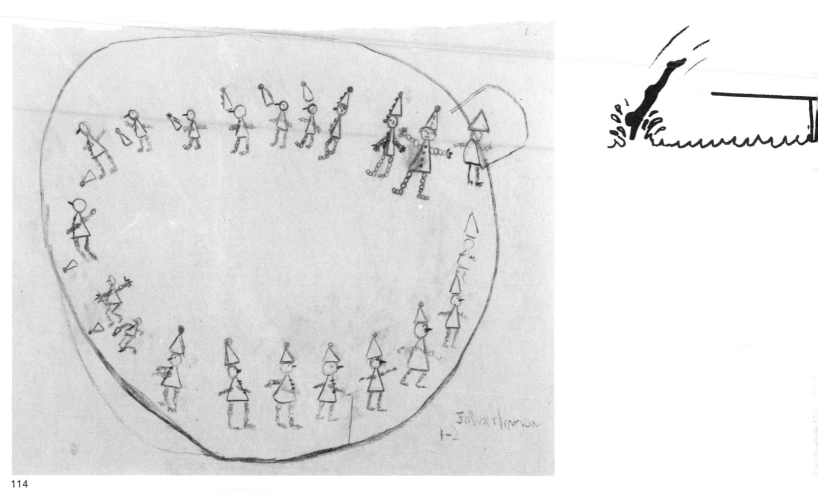

114

115

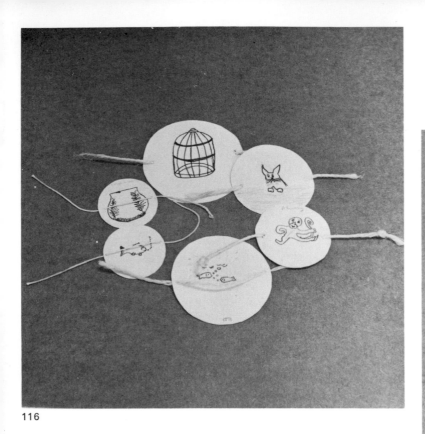

116

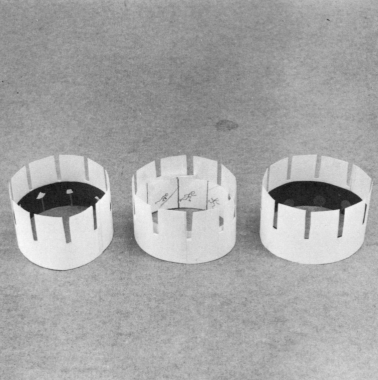

117

running along the top right-hand pages of this book where it can actually be flipped. As an introduction to the moving image, other simple mechanical devices can be made, such as the zoetrope and flip discs shown here where figurative and non-figurative elements may be exploited.

Ideally these basic techniques should act as an introduction to the use of film itself, but where this is impossible then study sessions around selected sequences from commercial films can be the follow-up. Some of the fundamental aspects of film and television can be explored in this way, but a large number of schools already have equipment for producing short cinefilms. An increasing number of schools also possess closed-circuit television equipment.

We have been looking briefly at some experiences in the art room which are directly related to the products of industrial society, in the form of objects or communication. It should be obvious that the ultimate educational importance of these experiences is not in the production and testing of design solutions themselves, but in the development of understanding.

In the same way that a general art education in secondary schools is not primarily concerned with the training of fine artists, design studies are not intended to be specialist training for designers. If the raising of design standards is to be one result of this approach it will come about indirectly through the mass pressures of informed opinion and choice, and directly by providing a firmer vocational basis for those who eventually become designers.

We have so far looked mainly at practical activities which can encourage young people to synthesize informed judgements on design products. In all cases there is a need to apply this understanding to a critical design analysis of the urban – or rural – environment. This can take place in follow-up activities where, through research and discussion centred upon actual products, visits and case histories, the young person's ideas can develop.

72

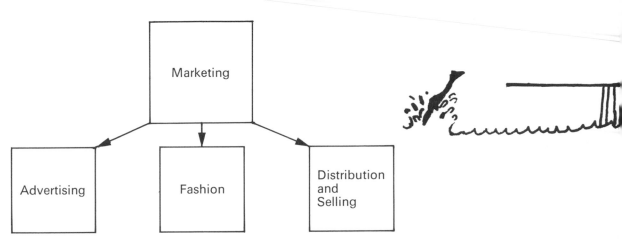

Marketing

Advertising | Fashion | Distribution and Selling

118

Marketing

Advertising

The dramatic increase in mass-marketing methods has produced a tightly woven mesh of confusing pressures on the individual. It is becoming increasingly more difficult for people to distinguish between the reality of a product and the image of it projected by advertising and selling techniques. The aim of the work with children in this area is to enable the adolescent, at whom much advertising pressure is being directed, to develop powers of discrimination through an understanding of what is going on.

The practical study of the methods of the advertiser follows naturally from the investigations of communication which have just been described. The emphasis here, however, is on the ways in which particular elements of mass visual communication are manipulated to become the tools of mass visual persuasion. Examples of this are the exploitation of an individual's conscious and sub-conscious response to social class, sex and acquisitiveness.

119

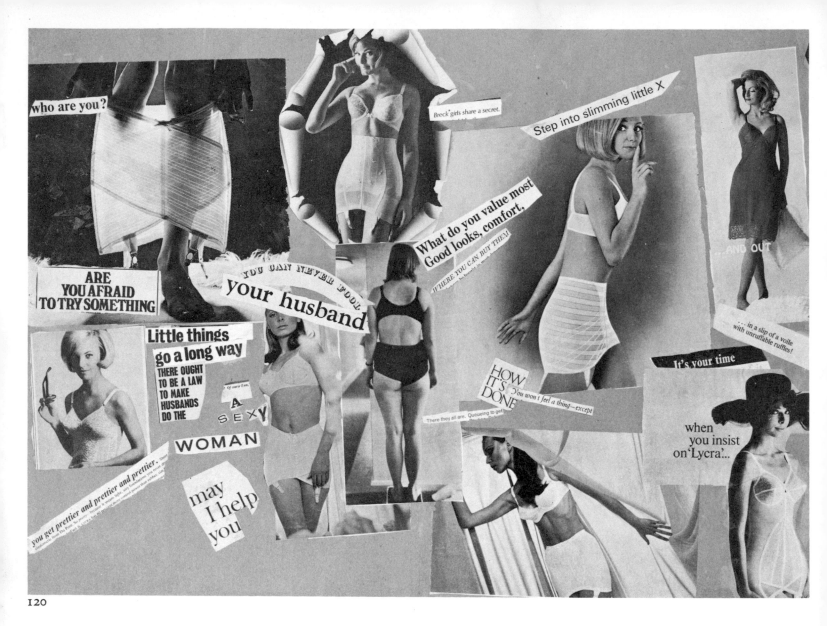

120

121

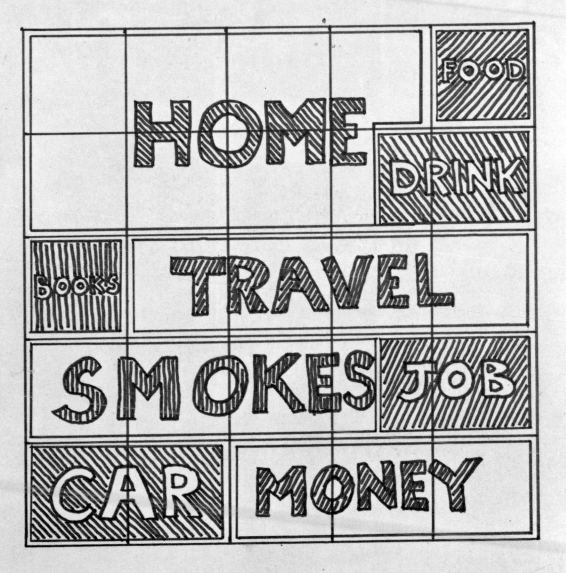

THE SUNDAY TIMES

HOME

FOOD

DRINK

BOOKS

TRAVEL

SMOKES JOB

CAR MONEY

···· out of 25 pages of advertising

One way of approaching this aspect is to isolate the elements and then rearrange them to form another image. The collages shown here are children's attempts to use these elements to make a comment on the advertiser's methods (figs. 119–20).

Analysis of advertising in magazines and newspapers (figs.121, 122) can be carried out as an investigation of the relative amounts of space allocated for various products and services. In the examples shown this has been carried out in a two-stage process of collecting the information and then finding an efficient means of visually communicating it. There are many possible variations on this procedure – for example, finding out the quantity of advertising given to a particular product, or simply listing the basic elements used to sell different products.

123

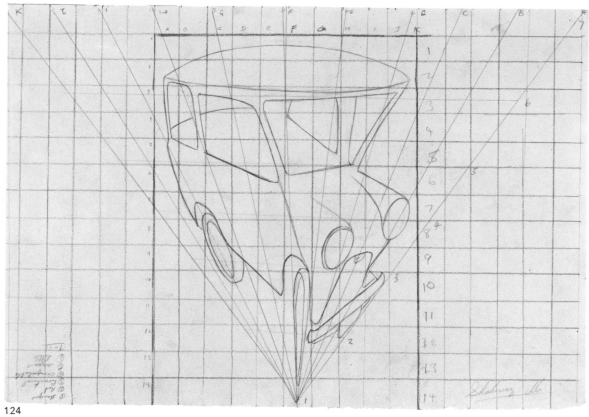

124

125

126

These are examples of work from a school where the children were finding out about the visual distortions used in advertisements related to cars. First an analysis was made, then this was followed by work using formal methods to exaggerate the existing distortions.

Studies in depth can be usefully carried out by smaller groups over a long period. Using a carefully prepared brief the examination of advertising can be extended to cover that shown on television at home or on film in the cinema. Again the idea of the scrap-book principle can become an efficient method of collecting a dossier of analytical information on the advertising used to sell designed products.

An investigation of the factors which give rise to fashion is fundamental to the understanding of the rapid acceleration of change in products of all kinds.

Having developed an understanding of the role of the designer and manufacturer, it is possible to carry out design analysis of products. This can be achieved by a study of the historical development of a particular item, or by a comparative analysis of several contemporary solutions to very similar design problems. In this way it is possible to isolate the changes which have taken place due to the application of new technology or materials from those which have come about through the developing patterns of fashion.

Another aspect of fashion is the use of styling. Two of the most obvious examples of this are seen in clothes and cars. Here stylistic changes create the desire to replace products long before their utilitarian function has ended. A logical step from this has been to design into products a predetermined length of working life which coincides more closely with stylistic changes. The concept of planned obsolescence is now even found in architecture which has traditionally provided a framework of continuity, stability and familiarity.

In both of these cases the products still look as if they are designed to last – the factor of obsolescence is subtly hidden. A more recent development is to design products with an undisguised shorter life – disposable furniture, paper clothes, cardboard houses.

School study groups on these topics will help the individual to understand the concept of fashion and change. The young person can be helped to come to terms with a way of living which is not based on mere greed, but is deeply rooted in the economic and social pressures of contemporary life. This seems a more positive step educationally than to look nostalgically for a non-existent traditional stability.

A study of distribution and selling methods again reveals a pattern of development closely associated with mass communication and advertising. The revolution in terms of selling through the super-

Fashion

Distribution and Selling

77

market and other large retail outlets has produced methods of distribution which contrast sharply with the social traditions of the corner shop. Point of sale advertisements, free gifts and carefully manipulated display arrangements all apply the final pressure to push the shopper into deciding to buy.

127

128

   The exercises above in the design of packages, carried out by first-year children, are examples of investigation into point of sale advertising as a marketing method. The project included both the three- and two-dimensional aspects of container design.

129

These two structures are examples of an approach to the study of particular buying situations. The children were asked to construct three-dimensional images which communicated the overall quality of a particular situation, without any verbal description. The bank and the supermarket show a developed awareness of the way in which simple elements can be manipulated to project a particular image.

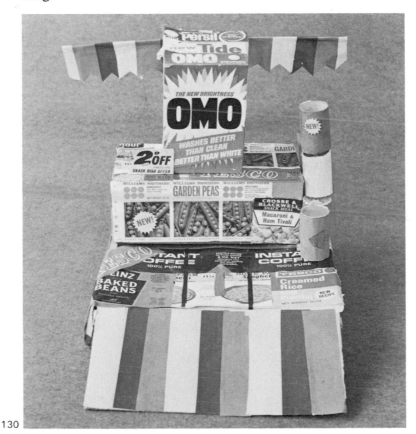

130

The examination of the pressures of marketing requires an understanding of techniques that can be used to make an analytical documentation. Immediate forms of direct visual study can include drawing, still-photography and cinefilm. Tape recordings can avoid the laborious process of gathering and analysing masses of statistics. The collection of such information, its analysis and communication to the whole class in a logical form can become an educational experience in its own right.

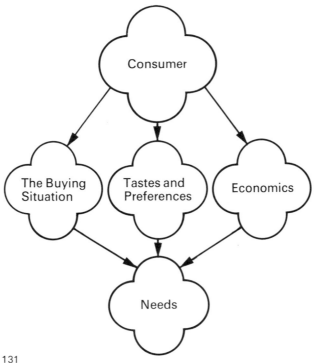

131

It is here, with the consumer, that we return to the specific problems of the individual. The question remains: 'In addition to an understanding of how and why designed products exist as they do, what else affects individual choice and discrimination?' Part of the answer lies with the individual's reaction to change in the buying situation, domestic economics, learned tastes and preferences and lastly needs.

It is sometimes too easy to think of consumers as being a separate group of people *in* society; we are all consumers – the designer, manufacturer, advertiser, salesman, teacher and child. In the school situation educationists are growing more aware of a complete subdivision of consumers – the teenagers. The comparative wealth of young people has given rise to a mass of products, advertising pressures and salesmanship aimed particularly in their direction. In a way consumer education for the teenager is more like learning to drive a car in heavy traffic than, for example, absorbing at leisure a piece of higher mathematics which may be used in later life. This is an indication of the urgency for educational measures to be taken now.

Studying the buying situation involves looking at the consumer's response to changing methods of distribution and selling, and follows on from the study of marketing methods.

Many recent developments have resulted in changes in life-long shopping habits. The siting of shops in building developments, in over-spill areas and housing estates can be contributory factors to the breakdown of community life which sometimes occurs in these new neighbourhoods. Self-service is beginning to apply to the selling of many commodities which have until now been sold in a more personal way.

These changes will probably be responsible for the emergence of new sets of prejudices which will, in turn, be exploited by new marketing methods. In school it is important that we begin to examine the effects on the consumer of changing shopping conditions. Some consumers have withdrawn from what has for them become a confusing situation and this has led to a rapid increase in mail-order business and door-to-door selling using particularly ruthless methods.

Tastes and Preferences

The development of tastes and preferences is the result of a complex interaction of social and psychological factors. The influence of parents and social class imposes traditional likes and dislikes which the young person may accept or reject – as demonstrated in these examples (figs.132–134) taken from school work on interior-design preferences.

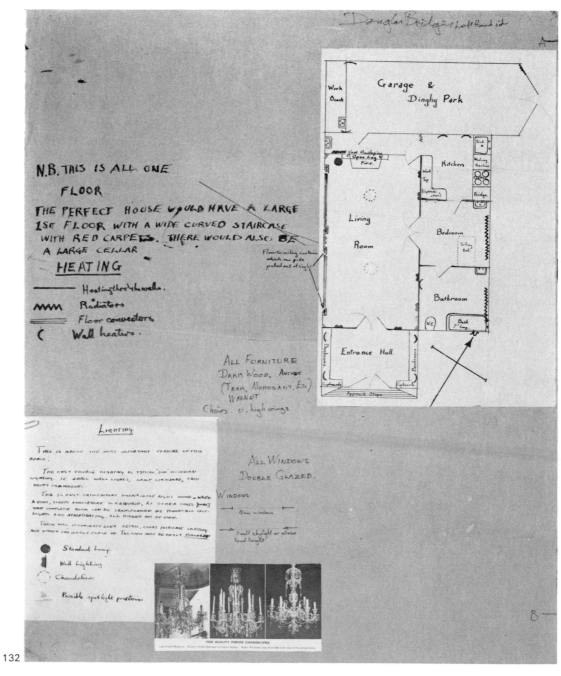

132

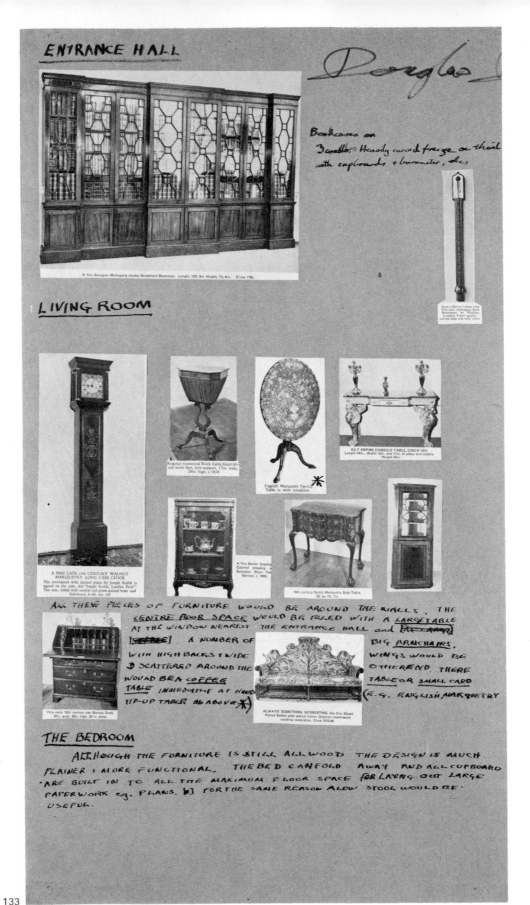

ENTRANCE HALL

Douglas

Bookcases on
3 walls. Heavily carved frieze on third
with cupboards + barometer, etc.

A fine Georgian Mahogany double Breakfront Bookcase. Length, 12ft. 8in. Height, 7ft. 8in.   Circa 1780.

Rare collector's piece: mid 17th cent. mahogany Stick Barometer by Whitehurst, London. Finest quality carved edge and tube cover.

LIVING ROOM

A FINE LATE 17th CENTURY WALNUT MARQUETRY LONG CASE CLOCK
The movement with limbed plates by Joseph Knibb is signed on the case, dial "Joseph Knibb, Londini Fecit". The case, inlaid with natural and green stained bone and fruitwood, is 6ft. 6in. tall.

Regency rosewood Work Table fitted lift-out work box, lyre support, 17in. wide, 29in. high, c.1810

English Marquetry Tip-Up Table in mint condition

GILT EMPIRE CONSOLE TABLE, CIRCA 1810
Length 54in., Width 19in. and 17in. at sides and middle. Height 34in.

A fine Boulle Display Cabinet showing a Georgian Silver Tea Service, c. 1820.

18th century Dutch Marquetry Side Table, 3ft. by 1ft. 7in.

ALL THESE PIECES OF FURNITURE WOULD BE AROUND THE WALLS. THE
CENTRE FLOOR SPACE WOULD BE FILLED WITH A LARGE TABLE
AT THE WINDOW NEAREST THE ENTRANCE HALL and [SETTEE]
[SETTEE] A NUMBER OF   BIG ARMCHAIRS.
WITH HIGH BACKS + WIDE   WINGS WOULD BE
⊃ SCATTERED AROUND THE   OTHER END. THERE
WOULD BE A COFFEE   TABLE OR SMALL CARD
TABLE IMMEDIATELY AT HAND   (E.G. ENGLISH MARQUETRY
TIP-UP TABLE AS ABOVE *)

Fine early 18th century oak Bureau Desk, 30in. wide, 38in. high, 20 in. deep.

ALWAYS SOMETHING INTERESTING, like this Stuart Period Settee with walnut frame. Original needlework needling restoration. Circa 1670-80.

THE BEDROOM

ALTHOUGH THE FURNITURE IS STILL ALL WOOD THE DESIGN IS MUCH
PLAINER + MORE FUNCTIONAL. THE BED CAN FOLD AWAY AND ALL CUPBOARD
ARE BUILT IN TO ALL THE MAXIMUM FLOOR SPACE FOR LAYING OUT LARGE
PAPERWORK e.g. PLANS. FOR THE SAME REASON A LOW STOOL WOULD BE
USEFUL.

133

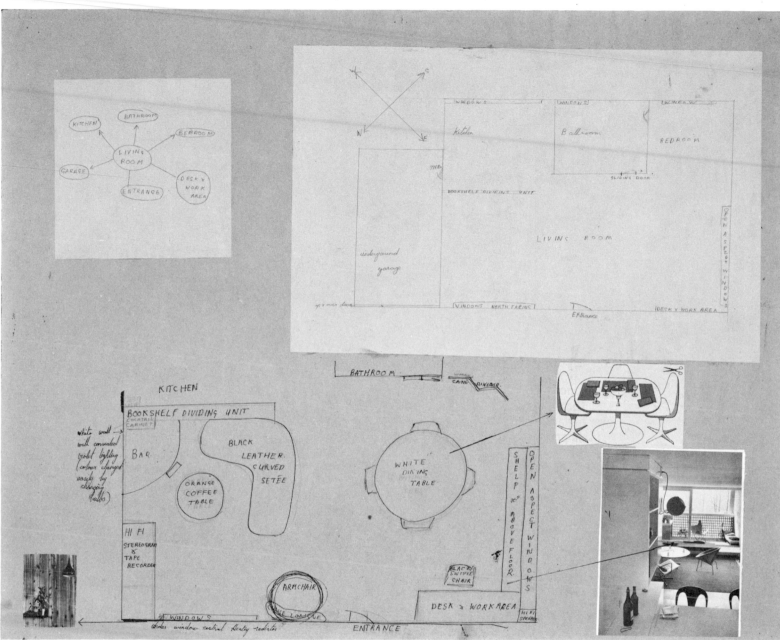

134

Our everyday environment tends to condition our thinking in terms of range of choice and nature of selection. This kind of conditioning can be at least as subtle as the pressures of advertising and the mass media. It can provide the foundation for many irrational elements involved in choice and discrimination. In analysing the buying situation, tastes and preferences, the art room facilities present the possibility of using direct visual methods. In the light of the experience and ability of the school child this direct method of documentation has distinct advantages over the preparation of lengthy and largely misinterpreted questionnaires and masses of statistical information. In this way complex problems can be studied as a lively area of practical experience.

An understanding of the systematic methods of the designer for solving complex problems can be used in the sphere of consumer economics. Domestic budgeting has become very involved since developments in standardization, planned obsolescence and throw-away commodities. The competing needs for change and stability require planning on a long- and short-term basis. The economics of buying several cardboard chairs instead of one of the solid traditional type is just one example of the enormous and very varied range of possibilities that now exist.

The collection and analysis of relevant information can become the subject matter for an exercise

Economics

Needs

in visual communication, where the relative economic merits of one set of choices can be compared with another. Comparative studies of prices at local shops and the examination of the historical development of price changes for a particular product can also be a valid part of the investigation.

An enquiry into the real needs of the consumer should be the culmination of all that has gone before.

Group studies, discussions and communication exercises can evolve from the problem of evaluating the real needs of individuals as young people and the predicted requirements of adult life. One approach is to begin by simply listing products in order of priority; for example, absolutely necessary, necessary, desirable, luxury, and so on, in terms of mental and physical survival. Again the process includes data collection, analysis and communication.

In this way much of what may have been hidden in the past, or only superficially examined, can be treated in a rational, objective manner leading to the expression of real individual needs.

It will by now be clear just how complex some aspects of life have become for the consumer. At present it looks as though study of this aspect to any depth needs to be carried out with older children. This does not rule out attempts in other situations, but since a useful and profound examination will depend on the ability to relate all the factors described in the previous sections, it should probably occupy a place towards the end of the teaching programme.

Conclusion

This has only been a brief survey of some aspects of the re-orientation of art education towards the problems inherent in the kind of society which exists today.

The hope is that the proposed additions to the present syllabus will make it possible to communicate their validity in a way that has up to now been difficult. The opportunity exists to develop in secondary schools a visual and design education which fits the pattern of a modern curriculum. One result of this would be that visual and design education could achieve a central role in the school, where in the past it has so often been neglected.

It is hoped that the simple approaches involved in the teaching programmes described here will be taken as evidence that these concepts could be put into effect in all art rooms today. Many of the ideas will be given an even more intense validity in those schools where co-operation and integration of departments are taking place.

The crucial test of design education in the art room will be its effect upon the individual's ability to develop a genuine reasoned understanding of the complex world of this century and the next.

Design Education in Practice

<hr>

5 CASE HISTORIES

<hr>

MICHAEL LAXTON A.T.D., L.S.I.A.

Michael Laxton is Senior Lecturer in Design at University of London, Goldsmiths' College. His contribution presents examples of work and patterns of organization from schools that have already succeeded in including design studies in their curriculums. In his opening section, he discusses general background problems and the possible content of a coherent design syllabus.

It seems important to preface these case histories of successful work in design education by some discussion of criteria, content and common problems. All the case histories offer something of value, but in the present developing situation it is necessary to see each one against a perspective of what could *eventually* be achieved. This is not in any way to decry what has been done. No projection of the future would be possible without the work that is going on today; achievements now are the essential foundation for a bigger growth of design studies in schools. However, I was so often told 'we are only at the beginning' or 'soon we hope to do ...' or 'if you could wait a year we would have done much more', that it is only right to acknowledge the existence of wider horizons and problems.

Need and Value

What are the specific tasks of design studies in school, and what opportunities do they give within the framework of secondary education? In the broadest sense, the impetus behind the subject derives from man's basic desire to make extensions of his physical and mental capacities and from his wish for a more acceptable environment. Thus, he has built houses for protection against the elements. He has produced power to give light and heat. He has developed transport to extend the physical limitations of his body. In our own time, radar and the computer have given new extensions to eyes and brain. The primary concern of design education must be to identify itself with these creative activities of man as an inventor and constructor. It must examine what, why, and how man has used the resources of his environment to construct the numerous material products of society. The extent of this approach to design should not be circumscribed by locality, but should naturally extend to embrace a wide field of social, economic and industrial problems. We need time in the school curriculum when we can examine the processes that are used to produce and construct the physical world we live in.

In a technological society science is the mother of invention, and design plays a vital role in determining how and when man shall benefit. On these grounds alone, a broadly based understanding of design is a prerequisite if the full potential of industrialization and urbanization is to be realized. But design studies have specific educational advantages as well. When we look more closely at the meaning of education in terms of a child's progress and growth we find the varying definitions leading us in a certain direction – 'to bring out'; 'to develop from latent or potential existence'; 'to prepare for adult life through awareness of contemporary society'. There are common denominators here that probably bite near the truth – to *develop and prepare*. We know we can educate only through three basic media – the child's emotions, his intellect and his physical awareness. If our intention is to prepare the individual to take his place in a balanced and responsible community, then we must attempt to develop and prepare these three aspects simultaneously and proportionally.

The freedom of a democracy inevitably demands self-discipline and a capacity to evaluate; but as the pressures in contemporary society increase, so the preservation of the individual's integrity assumes a growing importance. In this context, the ability to solve problems rationally through evaluation and application is a valuable human asset. This has always been true, but today nothing less than the progress of man is dependent upon the development of this ability. It is here that design finds its distinctive educational role; for the essential activity is *to initiate and pursue by the rational application of knowledge and experience to a given situation*. In other words, to design.

Implicit in the idea of design studies is the educational value of individual participation and response – the necessity for the child to observe, evaluate and create. The work can be as various as the building of a wind tunnel, the cutting out of a dress, or the construction of a simple kite, but it contains the opportunity for the child to learn and act as a result of his observations. Trial, investigation and experiment are all steps in the logic of the design process. What is more, design problems are inescapably connected with the realities of human experience and activity.

Apart from these broad social justifications, design studies could have a good educational influence on the special difficulties inherent in the secondary school curriculum. At the moment we have an education based on subject specialization which promotes the isolation of knowledge and activity into compartments. The opportunity of relating subject information to meaningful activities based on reality is rare, and sometimes completely missing. The introduction of design as one of a number of unifying activities could pull together these isolated subjects. It could even reinforce them by its own methods of analysis and evaluation.

The addiction of education to a two-dimensional and basically literary mode founded on the acquisition of knowledge through book-learning is fortunately being reduced. The opportunity and efficiency inherent in a broadly based active curriculum is beginning to be realized. Design fits this pattern and the inclusion of design thinking and activity gives the basis for a three-dimensional education of some consequence.

Properly used, design education provides a tremendous opportunity to involve the child in an activity which is personally valuable in terms of development, but which is also of immediate relevance to the kind of technological world we have. At the lowest level it can provide the child with greater resources to withstand the more doubtful aspects of mass production and mass media; at the highest level it can help bring about conditions in society which would allow us all to work together in greater confidence and security.

Implications

Perhaps the greatest single point which follows from the role which we have just defined is that it is the *process* of design, the intellectual and physical experiences it offers, which are of prime importance. We are not here interested so much in the results of activity as in the educative value of the activity itself. In planning design studies which are relevant for children we have to accept criteria which are to do with the development of the child, rather than the development of the design. As we shall see in the case histories the two things are intimately linked, but from the outset there should be no confusion about which is more important.

The implications of a move towards the acceptance of design on this broad basis are far-reaching, and it is right at least to recognize some of the problems involved. First there is the need for personal honesty and self-criticism. The teachers involved need to have an unbiased view that accepts a curriculum based on educational validity, rather than academic worthiness or status. Our own subject has to be seen as a contribution to the total educational responsibility of the particular school. The problem is to accept different interests and abilities, and yet find a way of combining them into the concept of a total programme. The benefits of team teaching, which in this area are basic to economy and efficiency, cannot be realized without understanding and good will.

The areas most immediately relevant to the concept of design education are art/craft/handicraft; science/technology; and aspects of home/social economics. Each of these is concerned with the activity and ability of man to shape his environment. Each is already in some degree directed towards acquainting the child with the knowledge and skill to recognize and build his future surroundings. It would be dangerous and even retrogressive to try to isolate further which subject carries the major responsibility for design education for, as the case histories show, a number of successful but different patterns of responsibility already exist. Enough if these areas can recognize and accommodate the basic media necessary and can set their studies within the fields of design and technology. In most

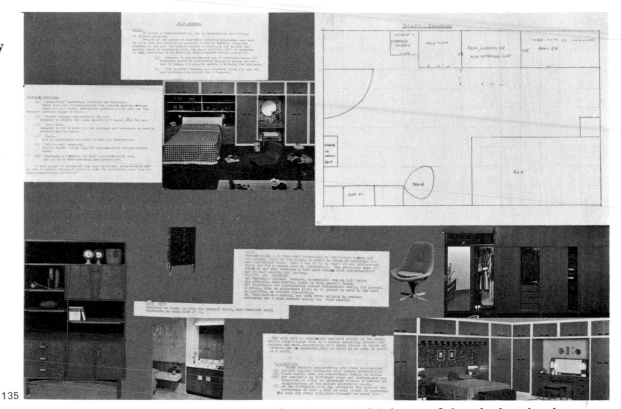

135 Design analysis sheet of a series of commercial products that could be used in a university study-bedroom. The sheet was produced as a part of the liberal studies industrial design course at the Cavendish School, Hemel Hempstead.

135

situations the three areas should be able to find a meaningful degree of shared educational responsibility, and eventually a common interest. This is starting to happen already.

The necessary degree of mutual understanding must also extend to the actual working situation. Much can be done in the most makeshift circumstances, but more ideally the environment for the programme needs to be specially adapted to accommodate the demands of the design process and related physical activity. The rigid specialist workshops and classrooms that suited previous subject fragmentation will not automatically be suited to the new approach. It will probably be necessary to have at least one multi-purpose workshop or centre, where work can proceed unrestrained by the limitations imposed by specialist requirements. For design evaluation and analysis it would be excellent to have a suitably equipped laboratory. A studio for preliminary design planning and discussion is another desirable facility. In addition, there would ideally be a considerable reference/information area, which would be more expansive than the conventional two-dimensional library. Its facilities would need to include three-dimensional reference material of many kinds, but with particular regard to mechanisms, construction, natural form, and a most extensive range of rigid, flexible, natural and synthetic materials. Within this basic accommodation a display or exhibition area of some size would be useful where, on occasion, simulated environments could be made and analysed as well as providing for home-made and travelling exhibitions.

The basic campus outlined is surely within reach, even without new building, provided we accept a degree of rearrangement throughout the present secondary school facilities. While a grouping of adjacent activities is recommended, they should *not* be isolated as a separate unit away from the total school environment, for it is basic that there should be the ready opportunity to cross-link and utilize any appropriate subject area in the school as a whole.

It will also be necessary to rethink our attitude to visits and activities outside school. This is an aspect that needs expansion and careful integration into the pattern of design studies. The artificial limits of the classroom/workshop must be expanded to accommodate the interests of the children as they arise out of a given activity. If we do not give them the opportunity to follow up their work by identification with the reality of life outside school, there will be little chance of holding their interest. They need to see industry in operation, and to be able to recognize the processes and patterns of manufacture. To see an automated production line at work should by now be as essential a part of a civilized education as is the learning of a foreign language. The experience of seeing a power station in operation, or raw materials being converted into steel, or wood made into furniture, can give the child confidence and understanding by reinforcing work done in the classroom. But the experience has to be carefully planned so that it is integrated into a coherent programme of study.

These requirements in terms of facilities and opportunity may seem considerable, but in themselves they will do little if the working situation is not suitably directed. The composition and balance of the design studies team will directly control the possibility of creating a successful programme. In the first instance at least, it would seem more important to collect people of similar attitude than to try for a range of persons offering certain subject experiences. If the team cannot work in harmony then the scheme is certain to fail. This certainly does not rule out individual enthusiasm and interest, but it does require humility and the exercise of trust in order to reach a common aim. There seems no doubt of the necessity to have one person who is finally responsible for the co-ordination and development of policy. This single director/administrator who can stimulate, unite and explain the aim of a group of inter-related studies, already exists as the driving force behind most of the successful examples of design education in this book. Often he has established himself as the head of a department and then, by sheer enthusiasm and hard work, has succeeded in carrying a whole group of people with him. This kind of role will continue to be an absolutely vital one in the future.

Looking practically at the contemporary school situation, it is easy to see that one of the major controlling factors is the time-table. Ultimately, inertia here can frustrate even the most lavish facilities and most competent staff. As with facilities and staff, the proper control of the time-table is a matter of principle, the more so because it has become a stock excuse for lack of energy and drive. It has dominated and now controls aspirations and hopes. Here priorities *must* be reasserted – should not the time-table be the servant of our aims rather than vice versa? The hallowed forty-five-minute module as a basis for time-table organization seems not only arbitrary but ineffective in its inability to satisfy the very varied needs of child and subject development. We might require, for example, a ten-minute exposition to stimulate a course of action, followed by a three-day period to intensify observation and involvement. In this context, the value of 'blocked time' and an established teacher/pupil ratio could well be investigated more fully. Within this pattern, we might use the ten-minute session with one teacher and 100 pupils – alternatively, we might settle for a three-hour working period with four teachers and twenty-five pupils each. The point is that the *nature of the project* should determine the utilization of time and effort, not administrative convenience. The freedom to structure courses and time according to needs could be the signal for fresh teacher involvement. It could also help the children who today often have to break off from an activity after a completely arbitrary short period.

Argument continues as to the correct age at which to introduce design problems, whether all ability groups can profit and whether girls should participate in the programme. Evidence seems to support the view that the earlier the process can be begun the greater the educational reward. At 11 years old the child's level of acceptance and curiosity is more readily available, and work can even go on before that in primary school. The question of intelligence levels poses problems of communication, stimulus and approach, but the child who has a poor intellectual/academic ability should not be excluded from a scheme. In fact, participation in the real and practical activity associated with the design process can be particularly effective, bringing a greater response than do more conventionally academic subjects.

The need to give girls an education in design seems obvious particularly because of their future role as consumers. This aspect is well covered by Peter Goldman, but it is important to remember also that all kinds of careers are now open to girls and that the job of a consumer is in this context simply an extension of the wife's involvement in homemaking. She needs a knowledge of house and interior design based on the exercise of critical evaluation and creative activity. A girl's day to day involvement with design problems is likely to be a good deal greater and more intimate than a boy's. Altogether, we can say that if we are going to start a programme of design studies, it must operate across the school spectrum and be applicable to all.

Realization

Given the accommodation, the staff and the freedom to introduce a course based on design activity, the problem is how to initiate a scheme that is educationally valid, practical and realistic. It is here that we can begin to ask – how is it possible to formulate and structure a successful programme? First we need a clear statement of objectives. A combination of previous examples, such as those in the case histories, and some thinking from first principles suggest the following as a valid list:

1   To identify design as basic to man's ability to develop civilization.
2   To provide opportunity for children to participate in decision-making and problem-solving activities within conditions of realism and objectivity.
3   To study the utilization of materials and scientific knowledge, in order to understand the manipulation and construction of the physical environment. From this to explore the constructive and manufacturing processes available to man.
4   To develop the ability of the individual child to discriminate and evaluate, through a growing awareness based on experience.

In all, to promote the growth of a society able to recognize the challenge of technology, and willing and ready, through the understanding of design, to accept and realize its promise.

The key to achieving the aims in our list lies in a thorough understanding of the educational potential of the design process, and its relevance to the various stages of a child's development. It is the design process that can involve the child's abilities directly and lead on naturally to discrimination or the wider understanding of the role of design in industrial society. It is less easy to work the other way round even though, at first sight, this might appear more logical. So, in discussing the development of a successful design studies programme, let us now look more closely at our earlier definition – 'An ability to initiate and pursue by rational application of knowledge and experience to a given situation.' What does this mean in the context of secondary education?

In order to work for an understanding of the design process, we must be able to describe its content and pattern of growth. Immediately it is possible to isolate three main skills:
1   Ability to initiate/express.
2   Ability to evaluate/discriminate.
3   Ability to interpret/translate.

136 It is possible to liken the skills involved in the stages of the design process to the three parts of a hydro-electric scheme. Each part is interdependent, but can be discussed separately for the purposes of analysis. All need to be developed if a child is to have a realistic experience of solving design problems.

These abilities are dependent upon one another if the design process is to be effective and it is a useful, if over-mechanistic, analogy to liken the skills to the three stages of a hydro-electric scheme – the reservoir, generator and transformer (see illustration 136). The first point here is that until the reservoir is sufficiently full, no power can be generated. The reservoir can be identified with the child's own breadth of experience and level of knowledge, for until he is able to draw on a personal vocabulary he will merely imitate or, worse, stagnate.

The composition of the child's reservoir and means of filling it need careful consideration. What is the basic vocabulary of visual and three-dimensional knowledge and experience? The answer can

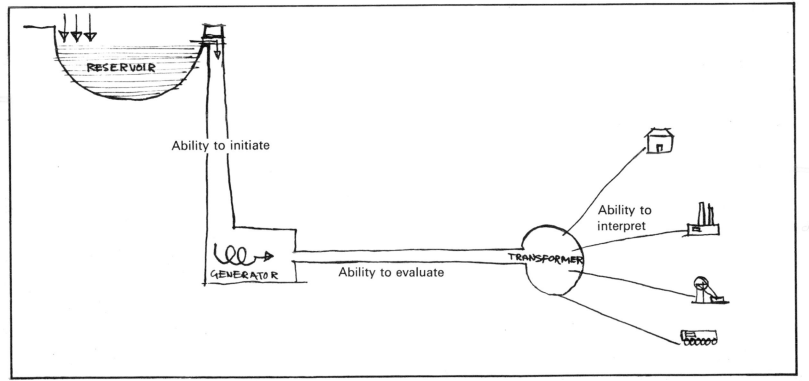

136

again be well shown in a diagram (see illustration 137). From this we can see that the depth of the child's reservoir is proportional to the wealth and range of his experience and the first concern of our programme must be to provide the opportunity to examine, explore, and experiment.

137 The 'reservoir' stage of the design process. The successful introduction of work based on the design process depends on the building up of the child's own reservoir of relevant experience. This diagram shows the ingredients and media involved.

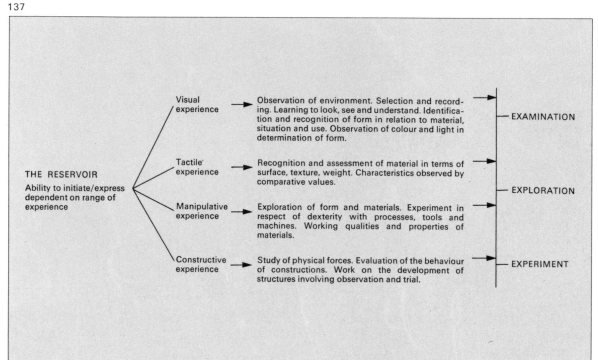

137

THE RESERVOIR
Ability to initiate/express dependent on range of experience

Visual experience → Observation of environment. Selection and recording. Learning to look, see and understand. Identification and recognition of form in relation to material, situation and use. Observation of colour and light in determination of form. — EXAMINATION

Tactile experience → Recognition and assessment of material in terms of surface, texture, weight. Characteristics observed by comparative values.

Manipulative experience → Exploration of form and materials. Experiment in respect of dexterity with processes, tools and machines. Working qualities and properties of materials. — EXPLORATION

Constructive experience → Study of physical forces. Evaluation of the behaviour of constructions. Work on the development of structures involving observation and trial. — EXPERIMENT

138 This diagram shows the ingredients of the evaluation or 'generator' stage of the design process.

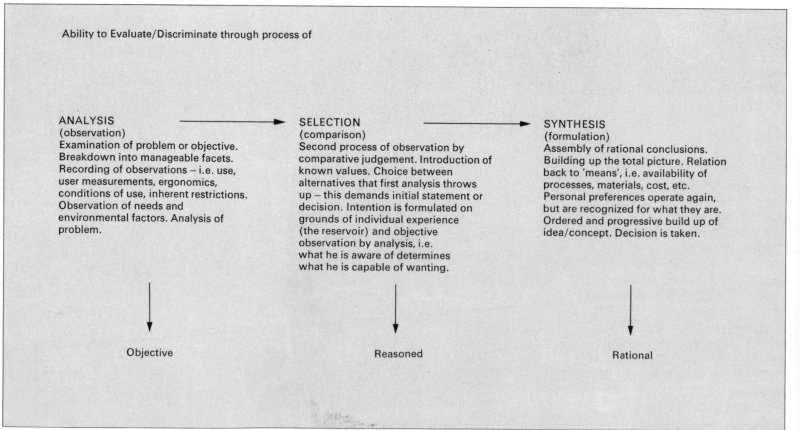

Ability to Evaluate/Discriminate through process of

ANALYSIS
(observation)
Examination of problem or objective. Breakdown into manageable facets. Recording of observations – i.e. use, user measurements, ergonomics, conditions of use, inherent restrictions. Observation of needs and environmental factors. Analysis of problem.

→ SELECTION
(comparison)
Second process of observation by comparative judgement. Introduction of known values. Choice between alternatives that first analysis throws up – this demands initial statement or decision. Intention is formulated on grounds of individual experience (the reservoir) and objective observation by analysis, i.e. what he is aware of determines what he is capable of wanting.

→ SYNTHESIS
(formulation)
Assembly of rational conclusions. Building up the total picture. Relation back to 'means', i.e. availability of processes, materials, cost, etc. Personal preferences operate again, but are recognized for what they are. Ordered and progressive build up of idea/concept. Decision is taken.

Objective   Reasoned   Rational

138

Motivation/Conviction

Personal need or challenge. Real
involvement necessary in order to gain
maximum motivation. Project must be real,
relevant and meaningful. Problem should
make use of gained information, experience
and ability.

→

Confidence/Ability, skill

The child must feel he has necessary practical skills.
Problem should range within his level of skill, be
demanding but not impossible. Confidence must exist
in his own ability and that of the teacher that they can
ensure success through a collaborative effort.
New skills can be learnt as the problem demands if the
attitude of confidence is maintained.

139

139 The final, or 'transformer',
stage of the design process. This
diagram shows the ingredients
that must be present in an
educational situation to allow the
child to transform awareness and
reason into a valid designed
object.

In the first secondary-school years, from 11 to 13, when we are giving top priority to the reservoir,
we should not be misled into adult concepts of finish or standards of achievement – these will come
later. In its initial stages the work should excite and involve. The aim should be to make the
first years full of new and varied experiences, waiting only for personal recognition and absorption
before moving on. This criteria would replace the one of manual dexterity which has often held sway
in the past in both art and handicraft.

Once the reservoir is being fed, it is quickly possible to begin to utilize its latent power, starting
slowly at first but gathering momentum as the confidence of the child grows through his own awareness. To enable the power to be used coherently, the next stage is to build the ability to evaluate and
discriminate. This is the generator in illustration 136 and it is an essential part of the design process.
What is involved is analysed in detail in illustration 138, and here we can see isolated the three main
facets of the evaluation stage – analysis, selection, and synthesis. The diagram should make clear
the educational value of the work involved, for it is in essence a training in objective thinking; it is
reasoned and rational.

With this ability in combination with the reservoir we should now be in a strong position. It should
be possible to take the next step and start work involving the ability to transform awareness and reason
into the solution of a given design problem. This stage is shown in illustration 139. Here it is absolutely vital that the projects or problems given to the children are realistic in relation to their own level
of interest, and also to the real world outside school. There is, for example, no sense in asking a 12-
year-old boy living in a centrally heated flat to design and make a poker. At the same time the complexity of problems needs to be carefully related to growing confidence and ability – challenging but
not so difficult as inevitably to cause failure and frustration. The formulation of suitable projects and
design problems is a key factor in the development of design studies and one to which the case
histories in this section should make a useful contribution.

We have, for the purpose of analysing the design process, isolated it into three main abilities. It
must be observed, however, that while these skills are necessary for the process to work efficiently,
it does not imply a rigid conformity to the three facets so far as sequence, allocation of time, or concentration of effort are concerned. All the same, it is perhaps possible to make some valid general
statement about the possible structure for a design studies course. In order to achieve the stated aims
through the design process, we can set down confidently some of the specific needs and criteria for a
practical programme:

1 Considerable opportunity to examine, explore and experiment with materials used by man in construction, building and manufacturing. Time to manipulate and evaluate their properties and potential. The range of materials offered needs to be extensive and not tied to any pre-existing subject boundaries.

2 Experience of fabrication and construction, through the use of the relevant tools and processes. Experience of contemporary industrial methods and technology through visits, laboratory experiments, and so on.

3 All work to be based on experience of evaluation, decision-making and problem-solving, through involvement in design activity.

4 All work to be based on the realization that in terms of education, the process of exploration, evaluation and experiment is more important than the exclusive pursuit of finished products.

To see the content suggested in this contribution laid against the five or six years of the child's secondary-school experience can help to interpret the accompanying case histories and to make a realistic statement of the possibilities. It will also focus attention on the very real problems of emphasis and balance that await discussion in the future. Illustration 140 shows a hypothetical balance of content related to the design process and the years spent in secondary school. Its aim would be to foster a basic understanding and awareness; the development of an attitude of mind that would be responsive to changing demands in society.

	1	2	3	4	5	6
The Reservoir — Ability to initiate	Maximum range of materials to be offered. *Discovery* to be main purpose of activity. Properties of material as to form, colour, working qualities, etc. should include: Clay, Wood, Metal, Laminates, Plastics, etc. Strong link should be made with art and geography. Emphasis on exploration through application to simple 'Child based projects', i.e. toys. Group work should be encouraged to follow up junior school systems of investigation. Quick completion of projects.	Continued exposure to material, now in greater depth and observation of application and method of use in environment. Emphasis also on observing the natural world. Forms and construction seen in nature. Projects should begin to show up the qualities and properties of materials in terms of strength and resistance to forming. Beginning of contact with mathematics and science. Projects still to be child centred. Group work still valid.	Attention more keenly directed towards structural considerations. Place of mechanics and man the engineer. 'How things are made'. The source and conversion of materials. Keener observation of architectural and art forms. Keeping of a Sketch/Record book should be initiated – this must from now on play a most important role, i.e. can be used to evaluate a child's progress. Domestic scene can now be used to sponsor projects.	Isolation of design as a process of man's activity as a builder and manufacturer. The designer, his work and responsibilities. Relation of work to history and pattern of contemporary society. Visits to industry, museums and local businesses. Opportunity to operate in society itself. Record books to assume greater importance.	Observation and opportunity to experience certain social conditions of work, commerce and planning. The beginning of an emphasis on specialization out of interest or facility. Examination of facets in this case in depth.	Explanation and experiment to centre now from own individual interest or ability. Projects should demand modest research activities, which take the pupil out of the school situation.
The Generator — Ability to evaluate	*Difference* of materials to be isolated by discussion, demonstration and experiment. Observation of 3D forms in environment used to equate form and material, application and use.	Continuing discussion and observation as to comparative values, properties and application. Pupil to operate in *choice* of material to related problem. Own statement to be based on personal observations.	The set projects will demand a more objective and rational approach. Beginnings of early analysis. Isolation of the problem. Use of record book to establish this regular pattern of rational thought. Set problems in addition to practical projects.	Analysis and comparative judgement begin to be important with particular regard to domestic items. Items of public purchase? Relate to personal needs: i.e. fountain pen, rather than pipe rack. Main effort to develop ability to evaluate a situation by rational observation.	Main concentration of course to follow pattern of problem-solving through isolation of need/use – user and situation. Appreciation of ergonomics, social implications and personal requirements. Ability to evaluate and discriminate in consumer products. Appreciation of value and cost. Discussion and debate to be encouraged to promote individual taste and discrimination	The main part of the course should now be based on evaluation and a process of synthesis. Course should be directed towards the pupil's own inclination. Strong emphasis however should be placed on consumer approach. Design and organization of social situation. Deeper appreciation of the creative arts. Organization of industry, place of design and technology. Strong reliance on record book to assess progress of pupil.
The Transformer — Ability to translate	Skills developed only in so far as is needed to complete project – limited range of tools and processes offered. Attitudes developed in regard to tools – care, respect and safety.	Increased opportunity to experience new tools and processes. Manipulation and relation of tool, process and task to be recognized rather than particular dexterity or skill.	Concentration now on the development of practical competence. Understanding of skill and its place in society. Machine tools should be used when available and appropriate. Attention to detail and standards. Technological studies begin to assume a growing importance.	Development of practical ability to centre on the understanding of process and techniques that arise naturally out of the given projects. Increasing observation of industrial method and organization. Consolidation of a personal attitude to work.	Practical confidence to be completed by strong demands and level of attainment. Still no attempt to 'initiate professional standards' but rather the practical work is used to provide the answers in acceptable form to the problem set. Specialization only to encourage personal interest.	Practical work should now be reduced. The design process which will proceed from analysis to drawings will include the making of models, prototypes, etc. Drawing, technical drawing, etc., will also be developed in support of the design process. Particular skills being encouraged in special cases of particular ability.

140 Suggested content of design studies related to the years spent by a child in secondary school.

St Audrey's School, Hatfield

The workshop layout at St Audrey's School is typical of many in Hertfordshire. The two specialist workshops are connected by a small design bay. The arrangement seems efficient and is approved of by the staff. Opportunities to work out ideas, to resolve problems by reference to a small library of information and to interchange between workshops are all allowed for in this way.

The practical work is based on the early experience being as varied and as broad as possible. Later projects are introduced as design problems and, whenever possible, the projects are suited to the individual boy and may even be initiated by him. As a result of this kind of approach the children develop confidence and self-assurance in the workshop environment and also an ability to rationalize a problem and recognize the disciplines by which it may be solved.

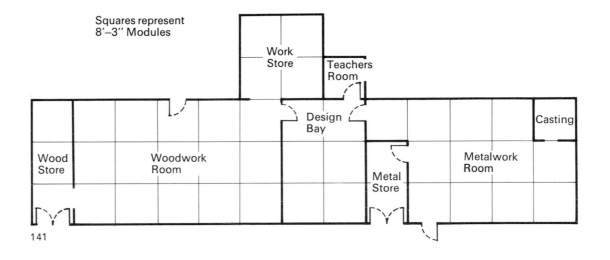

141 Sketch plan of handicraft workshops at St Audrey's School, Hatfield. The design bay is centrally placed between wood and metal workshops.

142 and 143 One use of the design bay is for objective discussion and analysis at the conclusion of a design project. Here a group are discussing and rating the merits of two dissimilar planes.

142

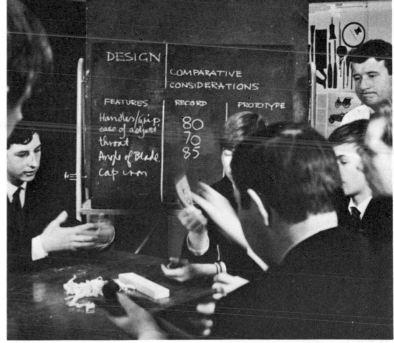

143

144

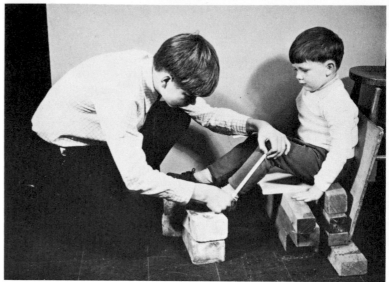

145

146

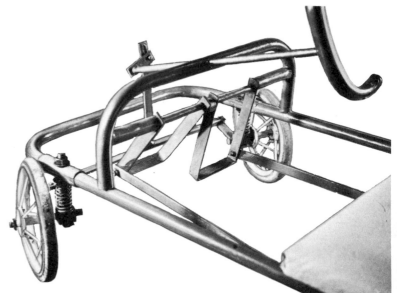

147

144–147 At St Audrey's, boys often initiate their own design projects. Shown here is a go-kart developed by a 15-year-old boy for his younger brother. Solving the design problems involved led him to an experience of ergonomics, elementary mechanics and engineering.

Case History 2

Wallington Grammar School for Boys

Wallington is one of the few grammar schools that give their art and craft departments an opportunity to realize their full educational potential. There is no Cinderella attitude towards practical work, and the sixth-form strength of the Art and Design Department illustrates this very clearly. The work being done is now recognized as appropriate for a pre-diploma course and students have gained direct entry into DipAD (Diploma in Art and Design) courses and to the Royal College of Art.

The strength and success of the work comes partly from the coherence of its aims. Mr R P B Wood ARCA ATD, head of the department, writes:

'Our aim quite simply is to teach the fine and applied arts as one subject while being aware that at their extreme polarities they may appear as separate things. We believe that in all art there is design and that in all design there must be art. In our organization of the course there is no hard distinction between the two-dimensional and the three-dimensional areas, yet each contributory subject retains its own distinctive quality. Each member of the teaching staff subscribes to a common aim and purpose; the same fundamentals are presented by each through his own personal and craft approach. From the start of any project, art, design and craftsmanship are regarded as indivisible, nevertheless each requires distinctive emphasis.

'We have implied that aims are inseparable from methods of teaching, and that in themselves they convey little; however, we should say that our aims in more specific terms are briefly:

1   To promote reactions to ideas, surroundings, and to problems of design through the use of all the senses.
2   To make a study of the various aspects of form and the fundamentals of design.
3   To provide an understanding and practical experience of materials and techniques and the relationship of these to design.
4   To produce work of an emotive and constructive character.'

The sketch plan of the department's facilities shows how the staff themselves have built an environment related to their objectives. It has been proposed that the accommodation should be enlarged by the addition of a metal workshop. This development would take the department a stage further in its aim of giving a 'practical experience of materials'.

148 Plan of the Art and Design Department at Wallington Grammar School for Boys. It is hoped that an extension for metalwork will be added shortly.

149 Boys discussing completed work in the ceramics studio.

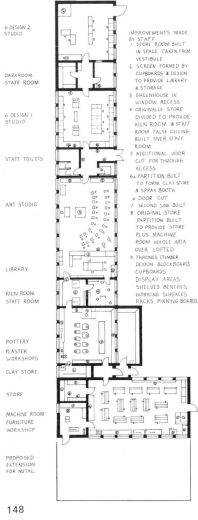

6 DESIGN 2 STUDIO

DARKROOM STAFF ROOM

6 DESIGN 1 STUDIO

STAFF TOILETS

ART STUDIO

LIBRARY

KILN ROOM STAFF ROOM

POTTERY PLASTER WORKSHOPS

CLAY STORE

STORE

MACHINE ROOM FURNITURE WORKSHOP

PROPOSED EXTENSION FOR METAL.

IMPROVEMENTS MADE BY STAFF
1 STORE ROOM BUILT IN SPACE TAKEN FROM VESTIBULE
2 SCREEN FORMED BY CUPBOARDS & DEXION TO PROVIDE LIBRARY & STORAGE
3 GREENHOUSE IN WINDOW RECESS
4 ORIGINALLY STORE DIVIDED TO PROVIDE KILN ROOM & STAFF ROOM FALSE CEILING BUILT OVER STAFF ROOM
5 ADDITIONAL DOOR CUT FOR THROUGH ACCESS
6A PARTITION BUILT TO FORM CLAY STORE & SPRAY BOOTH
a DOOR CUT
7 SECOND SINK BUILT
8 ORIGINAL STORE PARTITION BUILT TO PROVIDE STORE PLUS MACHINE ROOM WHOLE AREA OVER LOFTED
9 THRONES (TIMBER DEXION BLOCKBOARD) CUPBOARDS DISPLAY AREAS SHELVES, BENCHES, WORKING SURFACES RACKS, PINNING BOARDS

148

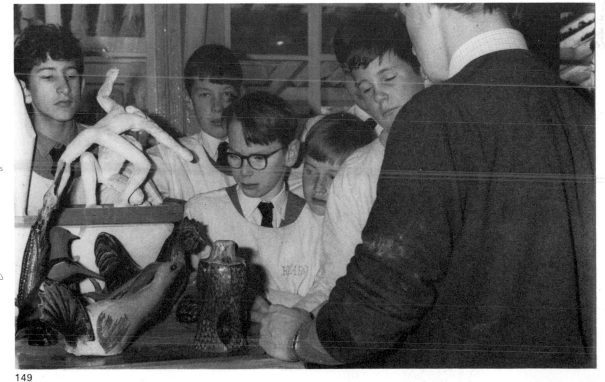

149

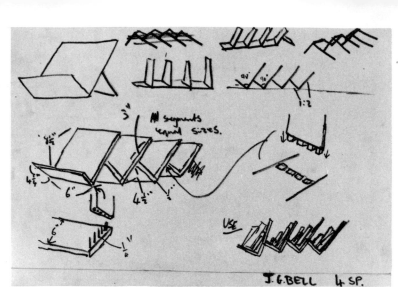

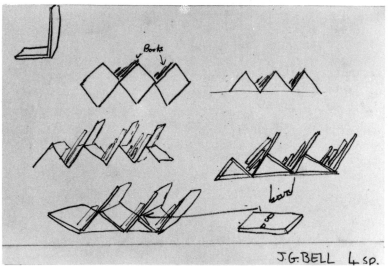

150

151

J.G.BELL 4 SP.

J.G.BELL 4 SP.

152

153

154

153–7 Other examples of work produced at Wallington Grammar School, all by 17- or 18-year-olds who have gained direct entry to DipAD courses. 153 Composition based on a wood module; 154 Mechanical form; 155 Toast rack.

150–152 At Wallington designs often grow directly out of experimental work with materials and not from a brief given in the first place. This book support, developed by a 14-year-old, shows how the approach works out in practice. By using a method of designing three dimensionally, using modules and seeing what they will do, possibilities begin to occur. From the three-dimensional sketch (seen beside the finished prototype in illustration 152) rough drawings are produced and from these the prototype is made.

155

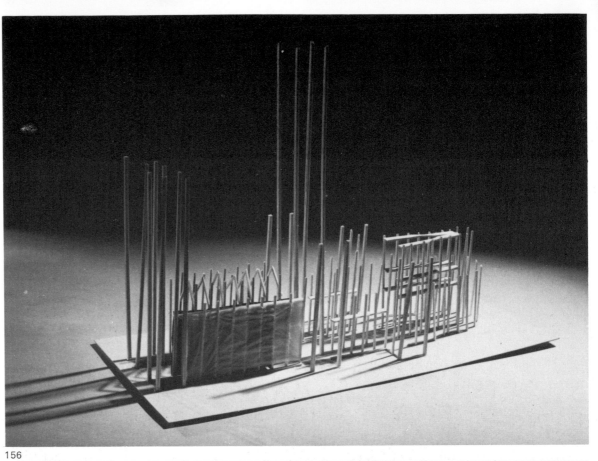

156 Concept of a cathedral.

156

157 Child's playground
structure.

157

98

Case History 3

Tottenham School

The programme being introduced into the workshop curriculum at Tottenham is experimental, but it is not a complete rejection of previous traditions and approaches. The significant change is one of attitude; there is a growing awareness that it is not the subject that is of prime importance, but the manner of its introduction and the experience it offers.

Using quite conventional problems, the staff at the school have redirected the programme of work so as to depend on an understanding of the design process. Problem solving is taken as the core of the course as explained by Mr C Larbey, the head of department:

'Too often children are put into situations in which they have no planning to do, or decisions to make – the problems have already been resolved by the teacher who has only to supervise the pre-determined method of production to ensure that the child will produce a reasonable facsimile of the original object.

'Our aim is to present problems to a boy that can be defined and analysed by logical thinking and group discussion. The extensive use of sketch books together with an examination of materials is encouraged so that the children may find their own individual solutions.'

158 Studying the ergonomic problems of a settee in the workshops at Tottenham School. The rig being used is a full-size mock-up in soft wood of the boys' own design.

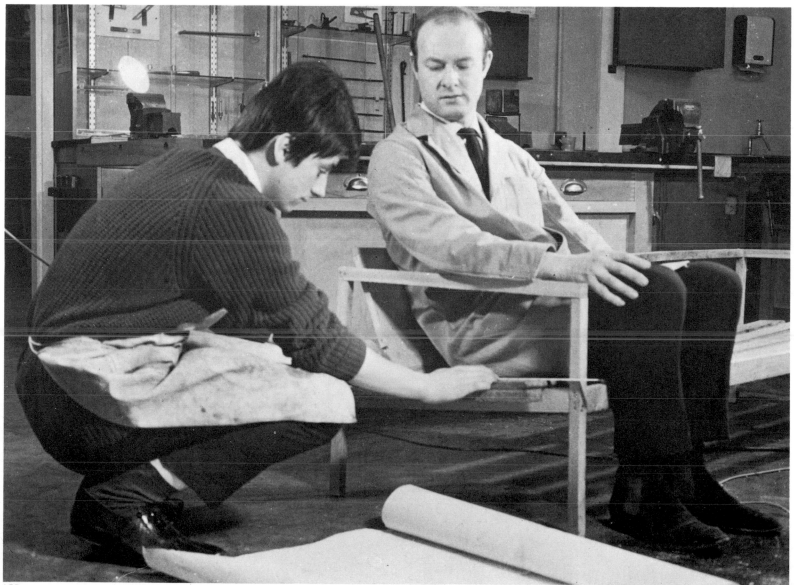

158

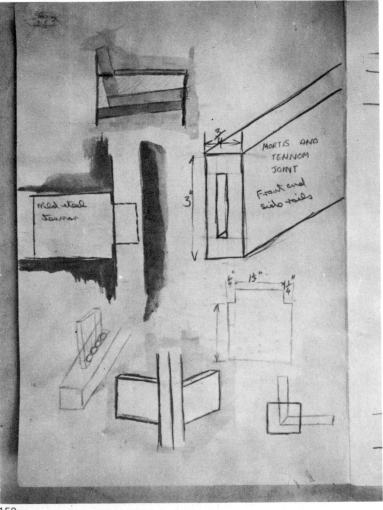

159

161

Page from the boys' sketchbook dealing with jointing methods for the settee shown on the previous page.

160

160 The joint under construction.

161 and 162 The tea-pot stand is a traditional subject for work in the handicraft department. Often it involves no more than the exercise of craft skills on a hackneyed and predetermined design. The same project at Tottenham starts from a careful analysis of the function of a tea-pot stand and goes on to the development of individual design solutions by each boy. Discussion of the finished products is an essential part of the work.

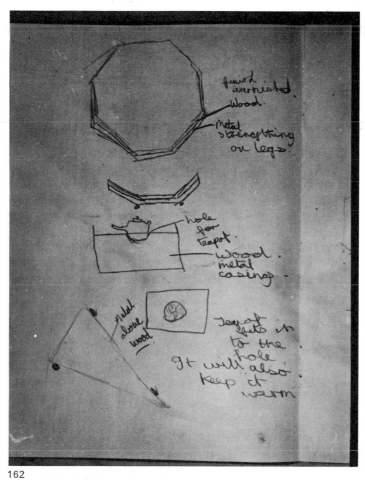

162

163 and 164 The variety and individuality of finished designs produced at Tottenham School are well shown by the results of this candle holder project (164 is overleaf).

163

164 Candle holders.

164

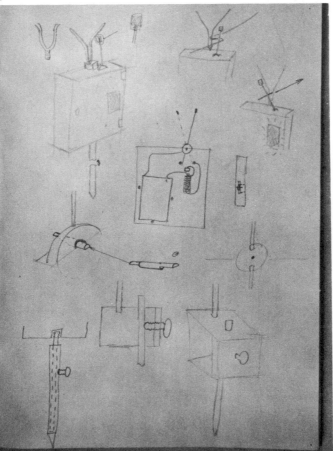

165 Page from a boy's sketchbook
showing the development of a rod
rest/bite indicator.

165

Case History 4

Orpington County Secondary School for Girls

Today wives assume a major responsibility in the everyday purchase of clothes and household equipment. They have an increasing influence on decisions about their home's decoration, furniture and layout. As a preparation for this major role as consumers girls need to have experience of the problems of choice and design in a society based on mass production.

In the art department at Orpington County Secondary School recent work has been programmed to help develop visual awareness and an understanding of design. A project frequently starts with the analysis of natural objects and leads on to the development of designs for fabrics or jewellery.

Simple design projects are tackled which involve careful statements of functional problems and the analysis of human dimensions and social behaviour.

Another aspect of design education at the school is the work done on the critical analysis of existing designs. In one example the girls examined their own handbags in terms of functional efficiency, durability, strength of construction, and so on. The depth of analysis surprised the staff involved and demonstrated how capable children are of making reasoned judgements when the opportunity is provided.

166–8 At Orpington County Secondary School girls are involved in work which starts from analytical drawings and leads on to the development of designs for fabrics or jewellery. In the example shown here a sliced pepper has formed the basis for an etched pendant (see also overleaf).

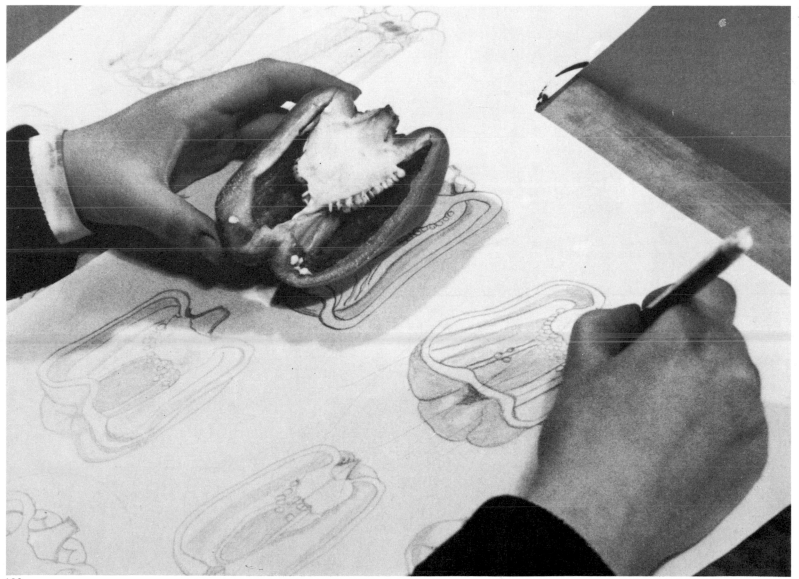

166

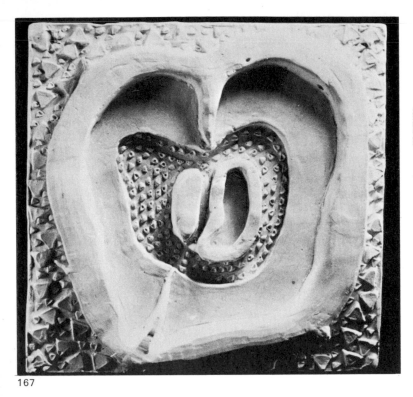

167

168

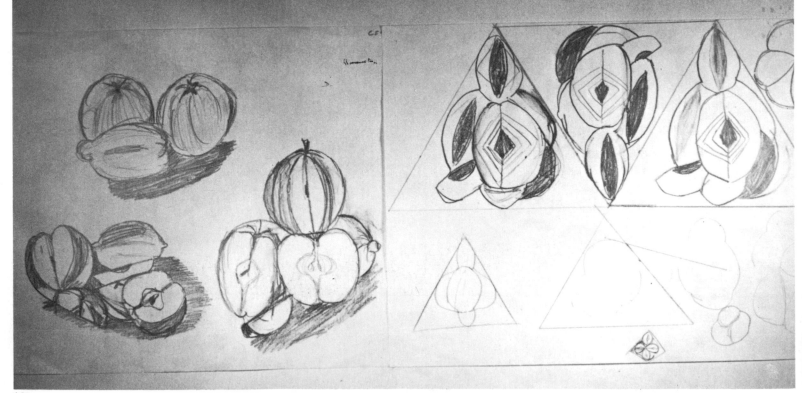

169

169–70 Analytical drawings of sliced apples used as the basis for screen-printed place mats.

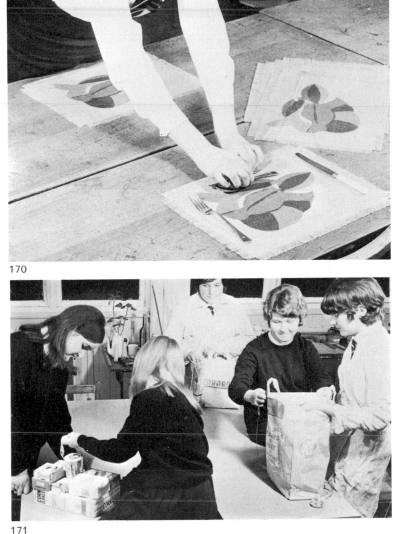

170

171–3 Simple design projects at Orpington are based on careful analysis of functional and other requirements. Here the design of carrier bags is being considered from the point of view of what will be carried and the person who will do the carrying.

171

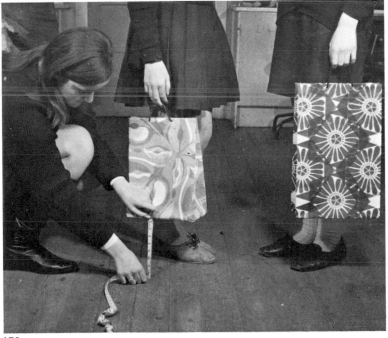

172

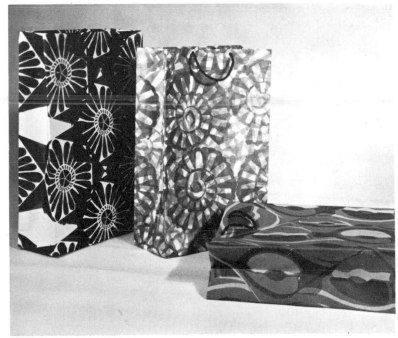

173

Case History 5

The Cavendish School, Hemel Hempstead

There has recently been much discussion of the benefits to be had from a craft course which is based on applied science. So long as educational criteria are kept clearly in mind such a course can be excellent. But excellence is not always achieved, and there is no value in simply replacing the old poker made to a formula with a new voltage tester also made to a formula. As is argued throughout this book, skills by themselves are not a sufficient aim and this is true whatever the orientation of the work.

The Cavendish School is one of the consultative bodies involved in the Schools Council's ambitious *Project Technology* which is directed by Geoffrey Harrison from Loughborough College of Education. Much of the work for the project is showing clearly how educationally sound technological problems can be, and a concern for technology is certainly central to the whole idea of design studies in school.

Significantly the basic belief of the staff at the school is that the children have the ability to reason and to design. Important also is the conviction that, from the first, contact with the workshops, tools and materials should be exploratory and not prescriptive. Projects range widely as staff attempt to introduce the children to problems and situations of immediate relevance. Mr M J Wharton (Head of Technical Studies) says:

'In a technological age when society faces a rapid cycle of change it is essential that schools endeavour to produce young people with enquiring minds, capable of creative thought, in a breadth of disciplines. In preparing them for life the knowledge imparted must, if it is to have any significance, be related to the outside world; more leisure and man's increased ability to create and control his own environment are factors which cannot be ignored.'

In this context, it is interesting to look at the projects illustrated, not for their expert craftsmanship or professional polish, but for the nature of the methodology involved. In each case analysis of the problem has led on to a rational design solution firmly based on knowledge and experience of materials.

Mr Wharton continues:

'Our design/engineering and design/craft courses are programmed to provide intellectual stimulus and effort. The acquisition of craft skills is to a large extent incidental and the work breaks out of the superficiality of workshop boundaries. It is our conviction that the challenge to create and invent is an efficient means of motivation, and certainly the results so far give us evidence of the real satisfaction and benefit gained by the children.'

During workshop periods a variety of practical activities are experienced as shown by the outline time-table (illustration 184). There is a good balance between applied science and more everyday kinds of design, and this is shown clearly by the existence of a sixth-form general studies course in industrial design. One product of this course has been a number of display sheets (see illustrations 135 and 186), which are the result of a careful analysis and evaluation of commercial products. It is important to stress the analytical aspect of the work involved; these sheets are not in any sense decorative collages but the communication of the results of research, and the suggested basis for design improvements.

174 Flow meter designed and made at the Cavendish School. 175–182 This series of illustrations shows clearly how important the methodology of design is considered at the Cavendish School. 175 and 176 Tensile testing machine made at the school; 177–182 Sheets from a boy's notebook recording design changes and other information related to the machine. All children have to keep such notebooks on a daily basis.

174

175

176

12.1.67.

Four holes were drilled and tapped in the hand pump base to secure the hand pump to it. A pipe was fixed between the reservoir and 'T' valve. Two blocks of metal for clamps were cut roughly to size.

The clamp design proposed a problem even after the work commenced on the project. We knew what size they would have to be and what size sample they would have to hold but did not commit ourselves to any definite design, for we had many. What we thought would be the best is shown opposite. The main theme to bear in mind during the design was that throughout the testing of a sample the two beams (holding the clamps) would not be parallel. Also the test sample should be kept as simple as possible, i.e. not threaded or drilled intricately. This reason is obvious for

177

20.4.67.

A British Standard 'O' ring was obtained along with the dimensions of the new piston. Work was then started on turning the new piston down to size from a circular rod of mild steel.

Work was also started on the test pieces to be used by the machine. The British Standard was worked out from the information shown overleaf.

27.4.67.

It was decided that a new pump cylinder was also necessary. This was because the original cylinder was made from a tube and in turning it down to the correct size, the cylinder was distorted. As the pump was a vital part of the machine and as any oil leaking

178

The piston head joint to the top beam did at first cause much concern. The main trouble was that as the pump piston rose it pushed the pump end of the top beam up, whilst the fulcrum end remained still. Thus the top beam not only had to support a heavy load, but on the very position of application of this load had to move. i.e. it could not be a rigid joint.

Our first design shown did not solve the problem adequately. Although the pin ($\frac{3}{8}$") was quite strong enough, we had our doubts about the piston head; for it was only $\frac{1}{8}$" in cross section on each side of the beam. To make matters worse the top beam would probably swing through large angles for ductile metals, meaning that the piston head would have to be milled very deeply.

Making the piston head any bigger

179

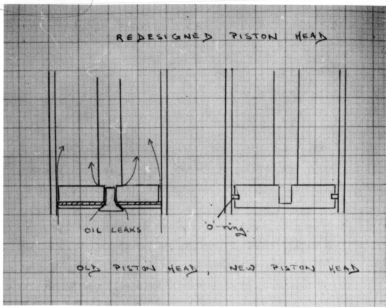

REDESIGNED PISTON HEAD

OIL LEAKS

'o'-ring.

OLD PISTON HEAD , NEW PISTON HEAD

180

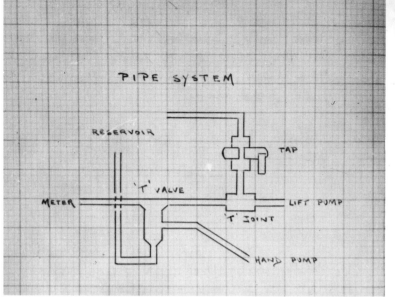

PIPE SYSTEM

RESERVOIR

TAP

'T' VALVE

METER

LIFT PUMP

'T' JOINT

HAND PUMP

181

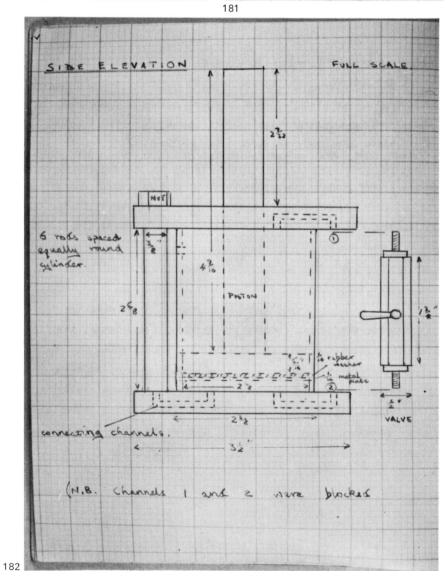

SIDE ELEVATION   FULL SCALE

NUT

6 rods spaced
equally round
cylinder.

PISTON

rubber washer

metal plate

VALVE

connecting channels.

(N.B. Channels 1 and 2 were blocked

182

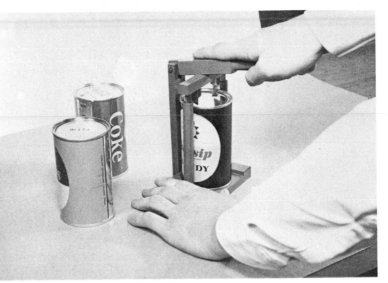

183 Device designed at the school for punching drink cans.
184 and 185 At the Cavendish School a deliberate effort is made to find a balance between technological and more everyday design problems. 184 Outline timetable for the Technical Studies Department; 185 Proposal (now put into effect in a modified form) for a sixth-form general studies course in industrial design.

183

184

```
2 YEAR BASIC COURSE IN
CREATIVITY AND DESIGN
A TOTAL CONCEPT COURSE WITH WORK IN DRAWING
AND DESIGN TOGETHER WITH WOOD AND METAL CRAFTS
INVOLVING 4 WORKPIECES - 2 WOOD/METAL. A DESIGN PROJECT AND RELATED DRAWINGS
IN THE SECOND YEAR 4 WORKPIECES IN BOTH WOOD AND METAL
WITH CONTROLLED AREAS OF 'REAL' DESIGN. WORK TO AN ADVANCED
STAGE IN THIS FIELD WILL CONTINUE THROUGHOUT THE YEAR GROUPS
```

INTRODUCTION TO THE MACHINE SHOP

INTRODUCTION TO PLASTICS.

CREATIVITY AND DESIGN - 3RD YEAR. LAMINATIONS. PROJECTS FROM OTHER DISCIPLINES.

SCIENCE PUPILS	ART PUPILS	ART/SCIENCE PUPILS
ENG. SCIENCE AND MATERIAL EXPERIMENTS	CREATIVITY AND DESIGN — WOOD/METAL/PLASTICS	HRS:- JEWELLERY ENAMELLING ONE TERM, THEN EITHER 1. CONTINUE ENAMELLING 2. WOOD/METAL CRAFT 3. METAL/WOOD CRAFT
DESIGN MACHINE ENGINEERING / MODEL ENGINEERING		FACILITIES FOR SPECIALISATION FOR PARTICULAR CRAFTS IE FOR/GLASS SILVERSMITHING ETC.
4 YEAR (TEACH)		
STAFF ORIENTATED ENGINEERING PROJECTS	CREATIVITY AND DESIGN WOOD +	CREATIVITY AND DESIGN METAL +
CONTINUATION OF MODEL ENGINEERING		
APPLIED SCIENCE AND TECHNOLOGY PROJECTS	ART PUPILS WOOD CRAFT ADVANCED WORK WHICH WILL NATURALLY INVOLVE DESIGN	PUPILS METALCRAFT PLASTIC FIBREGLASS ERGONOMICS DESIGN OF FURNITURE (MODEL MAKING) FACILITIES FOR SPECIALISATION

EXAMINATION WORK TO 'O' AND 'A' LEVEL IN TECHNICAL DRAWING
GENERAL STUDIES — VI FORM. - INDUSTRIAL DESIGN.
COMMUNITY SERVICE — WORKPIECES IN CREATIVITY AND DESIGN COURSES

JULY 12TH 1967

185

The course is to cover the progression from the drawing up of a design brief to the manufacture of the solution, through a number of predetermined stages, and to include visits/lectures by Professional Industrial Designers, The Consumer Research Council and The Royal College of Art.

Method of running Course.

A list of items of school furniture, domestic appliances and engineering components would be drawn up, e.g. A school desk, a tin opener, an easy chair and an adjustable spanner. The pupils would work in pairs and would select a Design Project from the list of items, and then work through the six progressive stages to a finished product.

STAGES OF PROGRESS

STAGE ONE.   A design brief would be drawn up in consultation with STAFF. This might be accomplished best by answering a standard set of questions.

STAGE TWO.   A number of existing solutions would be studied and apprised. The design brief would be presented by the 'Project Pair' to the group, together with their apprisal on the existing designs. Group discussion would follow.

STAGE THREE.   The existing design solutions would then be subjected where possible to a test under working conditions and a report given to the group.

STAGE FOUR.   A design solution would be worked out either together or each of the pair working from a different viewpoint. Working drawings would be produced after the design sketches had been given STAFF APPROVAL.

STAGE FIVE.   The design would be manufactured in the school workshops.

STAGE SIX.   The finished product would be examined by the group and conclusion made.

RECORDS.   A file in which all notes, sketches and comments would be kept would be maintained by the 'Project Pair'. Photographs would be taken if possible.

COMPLETION OF COURSE.   An exhibition of work showing the stages of progression would be staged by the group of all their DESIGN PROJECTS.
The layout of this exhibition could be a separate group design project.

OUTSIDE VISITS/LECTURES.

A preliminary visit to the Design Centre by staff to discuss the project with a view to obtaining help by way of literature handouts, arrangements for lecture/visit, and an introduction to useful contacts.

COURSE VISITS/LECTURES.

1. Lecture by a professional Industrial Designer at stage 1.
2. Visit to Consumer Research Association and lecture on testing technique and method sampling at stage 3.
3. Visit to the Design Centre.
4. Visit to the Royal College of Art with a lecture on some aspect of Prototype design. i.e. Three Dimensional.

186 Sheet showing the results of
analysing a series of domestic
electric plugs. The sheet was
produced as a part of the sixth-
form general studies course.

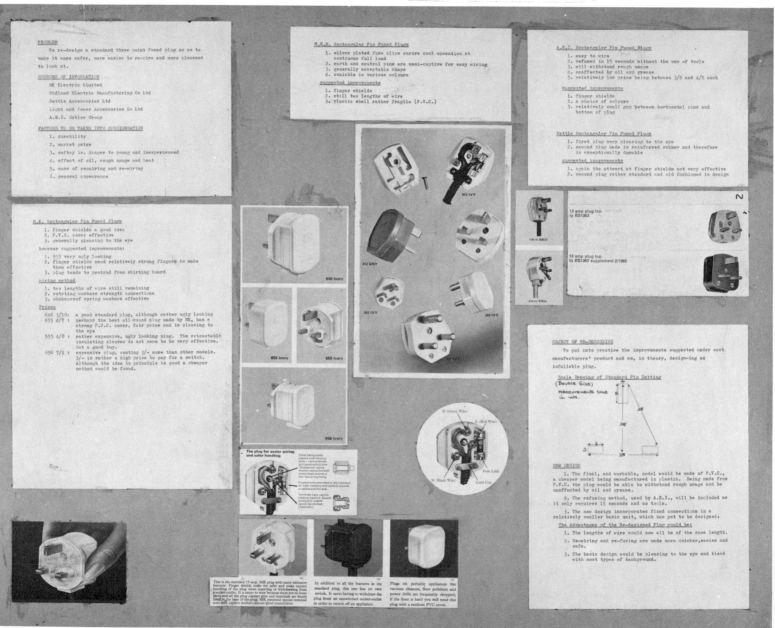

186

Case History 6

Inventions by Japanese schoolchildren

These three examples of inventions by Japanese schoolchildren are interesting in a number of ways. They show that the importance of design education is recognized in that country, as it is in a number of others. They show that relatively young children can produce highly sophisticated design solutions, and incidentally they show that national characteristics are reflected in designed objects.

187

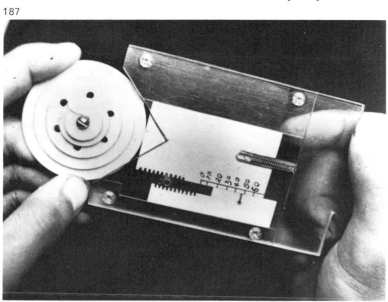

187 An apparatus for calculating the diameter or radius of round objects (such as toy wheels and gears). The indicator slides on a ratchet when the object to be measured is pushed into the V-cut. The inventor was 12 years old.

189 A floor-washing machine using an endless towel which revolves through a pail of soapy water with a brush to remove the dirt. The inventor was 9 years old.

189

188

188 Chart for recording daily temperatures, designed and produced by an 8-year-old.

Case History 7

University of London, Goldsmiths' College

As colleges of education are responsible for the training and supply of teachers, it is important that they are active in developing ideas about design education. There are indications throughout the country that this is becoming a major area of concern.

Goldsmiths' is the largest college of education in Britain and is probably unique in its composition, for it embodies not only a college of education, but also a school of art. It offers degree and post-graduate work, and has a large adult studies department. In the college of education, courses cover an extraordinarily large range of subjects in both secondary and primary education.

Within this framework, for teachers wishing to concentrate on secondary education, the college has a department of handicraft (design and technology) and it is from here that the examples shown are chosen.

The department is relatively small and its facilities are compact. Over the past few years it has been able to direct the course more specifically towards design studies. On entry, students begin with a foundation course. This sets out to develop a spirit of enquiry and at the same time to develop a personal awareness of the contemporary environment. This course is centred on directed observation and subsequent recording, both in practical and visual terms. Experiences at this stage range from aspects of materials technology to considerations of form and colour. The record sheets (illustrations 197 and 198) come from students' foundation-course folders, while the examples of practical work are evidence of experiments with materials. The objective problems that are given allow for freedom of thought and yet call for specific areas of activity.

As a conclusion to their first year work, students were recently given the problem of designing a simple press tool, which would produce a repetitive form suitable for assembly as jewellery. The first requirement was to arrive at a unit capable of being interconnected in a number of variations. Here, their previous work during the year was relevant and enabled them to recognize the nature of the visual problem involved. The actual design and production of the press tool took the students a stage further and reinforced their immediate knowledge of engineering and the behaviour of metals. The final stage of assembly offered the students individual freedom and yet again called for certain specific disciplines in silversmithing.

The project involved a complete experience of the design process and, in terms of student development, it achieved a considerable increase in awareness and individual understanding.

One of the big stumbling blocks to advances in the curriculum has been the various problems of assessment. The challenge is to re-think the purpose of examinations, their value and their objectives; then to structure a suitable system which will ensure the desired result.

At Goldsmiths' the traditional pattern became unacceptable in the handicraft department and an effort was made to develop a method of evaluation related specifically to the stages of the design process. Significantly, the aim is not to examine the residue of knowledge. Rather it is to find out what the student knows and how he is able to utilize his knowledge. The idea of discovering what he doesn't know and what he cannot do (the apparent intention of most examinations) has been abandoned.

The examples shown here (illustrations 202–12) are from an examination into the students' grasp of the design process which took place at the end of the second year. The project set was a toilet mirror. A brief was issued twenty-one days before the timed practical work session. From this advance information the students were to identify the problem, analyse its content and arrive at a design solution which could be produced in the twelve-hour practical session. The brief was issued in advance so as to allow the students to carry out trials and experiments, as well as to give time in which to prepare a detailed analysis of the design problem, sketch design sheets and full working drawings. On the day of the practical work session, the analysis and sketch design sheets were handed in for assessment and on completion of the construction period so was the working drawing.

The results of this examination are interesting in the following ways:

1   No two students' solutions were the same.
2   The degree of originality was high in construction and use of materials.
3   All had carried out an extensive analysis and had made sound and valid decisions. In some cases, the level of experiment was far higher than had been expected.

4   The examination became an event in which the students were fully involved, and was regarded by them as a logical conclusion to the year's work.

The freedom that was inherent in this mode of examination proved a valuable means of assessing a student's ability and understanding of the design process. It suggests that possibilities exist for a similar approach to examinations at secondary-school level.

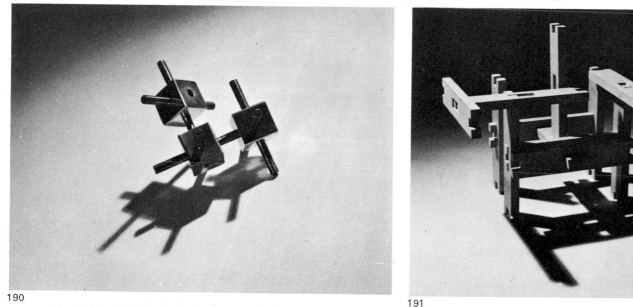

190

191

190–196 At Goldsmiths' College student teachers in the handicraft department follow a course with specific design content. Shown here is a selection of practical work produced during the first-year foundation course where the aim is to develop a personal awareness of the capacities of materials and technology.

192

190–192 Constructional toys.

193

194

195

193-195 Chessmen

196 Rearrangement of form –
cube cut and reassembled.

197 and 198 Record sheets from
students' folders produced
during the foundation course
(198 overleaf).

196

METAL - Properties and Potential

N°	TEST PROJECT	PROCESS AND OBSERVATION	CONCLUSIONS AND REASONING	EDUCATIONAL VALUE

Preparation of samples
Identical lengths of metal of 3/8 inch section are cut for each test.
The joint are on each sample is filed clean to remove the Oxides.

The T-shaped sample

The comparative testing of soldered joints

This is a comparative test of the strength of various soldered joints therefore it is important that the joints are comparative. Identical lengths of metal 3/8 inch section are used for each test. The methods used are:-
1. Soft Soldering.
2. Hard Soldering.
3. Brazing } one to be quenched one to be slow cooled

When the T sections are soldered the strength of each will be tested by using a Torque Wrench.
Then three samples of solder are to be placed on a strip of guilding metal which will then be heated from underneath so that the melting points of the solders may be directly compared with one another and with the colour of the hot guilding metal.

1. Soft Soldering
The bit was first tinned (cleaned in flux and then given a thin layer of solder) The solder is an alloy of tin and lead) The soldering iron was then placed in a gas heater until a green flame was emitted.
The iron was then tipped with solder which was applied to each surface.
The two surfaces were placed in contact and a blow torch was used to heat the T-unit. A soft flame was used and immediately the solder melted (about 250 centigrade)
The solder was applied to each surface.
Gas Heater
The solder is not meant to fill the joint. It flows by capillary action and the more it penetrates the stronger will be the joint.

2. Hard solder (Easyflo)
Easyflo in a wire form is applied to the joint when the joint reaches a certain temperature.
First Borax was smeared on the joint (Besides keeping the metal clean during heating this flux breaks down the surface tension of the solder and enables it to flow.)
Easyflow is in wire form, it is an alloy comprising 50% silver 15% copper and 19% Cadmium
The joint is heated to a temperature at which the solder melts (red heat – about 750°C.) The solder is dipped in flux and then applied.

3. Brazing (one joint quenched and one slow cooled)
The work is packed round with cake and firebricks to conserve the heat.
The joint is heated to a bright red (950° centigrade) and then the brazing rod is dipped in borax and applied to the joint.
The solder is allowed to melt by conduction from the metal and not by direct heat from the flame

A brick hearth

The TorqueWrench Test		
solder	poundage	Conclusions
soft solder	No reading obtained, very low.	Soft solder will be suitable only for joints that do not have to withstand pressure. A very strong joint because it appears that the higher the temp the stronger a soldered joint
Easyflo	70	This does not give an ample indication of the strength because the solder had strength.
Brazing	30	A joint comparison in strength to the high temperature needed to melt the solder.
quenched	70	

These tests are of Educational value because they may be used in the school workshop to demonstrate to pupils soldering and the relative strengths of different solders. If pupils can demonstrate to themselves these differences they may more readily understand them and then when they design or make anything in metal they may come to realise what type of solder will be suitable for the job.
Besides providing an insight into the different qualities possessed by the solder the test also has value in the workshop because it includes many of the fundamental principals of practical soldering. Thus the pupil may simultaneously learn to solder and learn about solders.

visual melting test

For the visual test three samples: easyflo soft solder and brazing were placed on a strip of guilding metal which was then heated from beneath.
Results: The soft solder melted very quickly even before the guilding metal had oxidised.
The easyflo melted when the guilding metal was a dull red.
The brazing metal melted when the guilding metal was bright red.
This is of educational value because it demonstrates visually to pupils. They can, for example, see the vast difference between the melting points of soft solder and brazing.

197

115

NO	TEST/PROJECT	PROCESS & OBSERVATIONS	CONCLUSIONS	EDUCATIONAL VALUE

5

TEST/PROJECT

The exercise here was to make a frame of mild steel, brazed together at the joints, and then to make the finished article aesthetically pleasing by introducing inserts of coloured tin plate, supported on wires.

PROCESS & OBSERVATIONS

On the last sheet we studied the relative strengths and melting temperatures of the commonly used solders and brazing metals. To put this knowledge into use, and to help to further develop our sense of design we made these simple metal frames, and filled them in various ways, with coloured metal inserts. The basic proportions for the frame were decided on after a selection of different shaped rectangles had been drawn on a sheet, (see accompanying sheet). By seeing a large number of similar shapes, it is easier to be selective, and reject the bad designs, than if there is only one example. For this reason at present when we want to design anything, we put down as many basic ideas as possible on a sheet, and select from them. Having chosen the correct proportions, remembering that the frame is three dimensional, we worked out the sizes for the material, to come within a limit of four feet of metal strip. This made the frames about six inches long and of end size two inches by three in this case, but other students necessarily had different proportions. The two ends of the frame were made first, holding the pieces of eighth inch square mild steel firmly in place by putting them on a powerful magnet, and squaring them up using an accurately planed piece of wood. (see diagram). These eight joints were made using brazing rod which melts at about 950°C. or at about bright red heat of mild steel. Provided that the metal was clean, flux was used, and the ends of the pieces filed square, there was little difficulty involved in this part of the exercise. However when the side pieces had to be joined on to make a rectangular prism, had brazing been used again, the original joints would have sprung apart as soon as the brazing rod reached melting point. For this reason a silver solder was used, and this has a much lower melting point, the medium solder we used melting at around 600°C. In order to obtain a more concentrated flame at the joint, an oxyacetaline torch was used, care being taken not to heat up the metal to the melting point of the brazing, (very easily done with such a fierce flame).

The inserts were designed on the other sheet connected to this project, using the same principle as for the frame proportions. They were cut out of tin plate, and held in position by mild steel wires about one sixteenth thick. Even the forming of the supporting wires was taken into account for the final visual effect. In order to give the frame and inserts more impact, because they looked dull just left as bare metal, paint was mixed to provide interesting contrasts in the middle of the frame, and the frame itself was coated in black paint to give it a solid appearance to hold the rest of the shapes inside it visually.

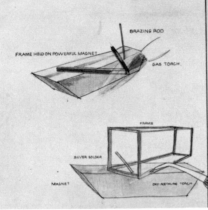

BRAZING ROD
FRAME HELD ON POWERFUL MAGNET
GAS TORCH.

FRAME
SILVER SOLDER
MAGNET
OXY-ACETALINE TORCH.

CONCLUSIONS

EDUCATIONAL VALUE

It would be foolish to expect a class of boys, unless of sixth form standard, to perform this project, and to get good results, mainly because they do not have the skill necessary for all the intricate operations. This sort of work on a simplified plan would however be most beneficial in introducing them to the new techniques, and also in developing some aesthetic awareness. I know that by the end of the sixteen joints using a torch of some description, and also a after soldering the tin plates on the frame, I am confident of being able to perform operations tollerably well, which until now I had not ever done. By making the exercise interesting, and giving the pupils a personal interest in the project (by letting them work out their own designs) Much more will be learnt, than by simply letting them follow a "teacher made" design. I suggest that a class such as would be taught these operations could be given some form of modern sculpture to design, using a limited amount of material. By doing this I am eliminating the necessity for accurately square joints, and allowing the childrens' imaginations to be used to the full. In this there is plenty of scope for jointing by different methods, especially if they are told to design the sculpture to make use of three different types of solder and brazing method. The results might be far more varied than those produced in these workshops, but the amount of thinking and practical work in them would be the same.

198
198 Record sheet from students' folder.

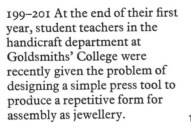

199–201 At the end of their first year, student teachers in the handicraft department at Goldsmiths' College were recently given the problem of designing a simple press tool to produce a repetitive form for assembly as jewellery.

199

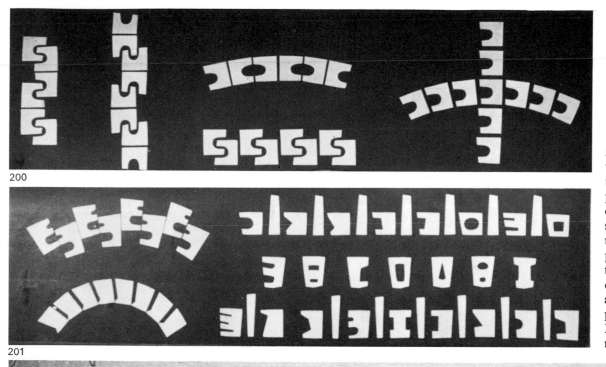

200

201

202–212 The form of examination used at Goldsmiths' for assessing the students' grasp of the design process provides a model that could be used in secondary schools. A brief is published twenty-one days before the timed practical work session. Based on this, students have to produce a detailed analysis, sketch designs and working drawings before the practical work begins. 202–204 Design analysis sheets for toilet mirror.

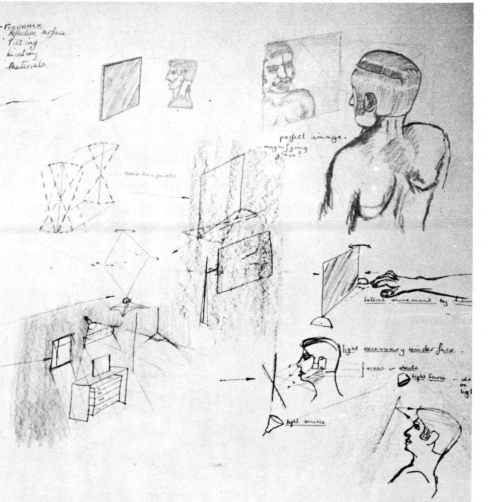

202

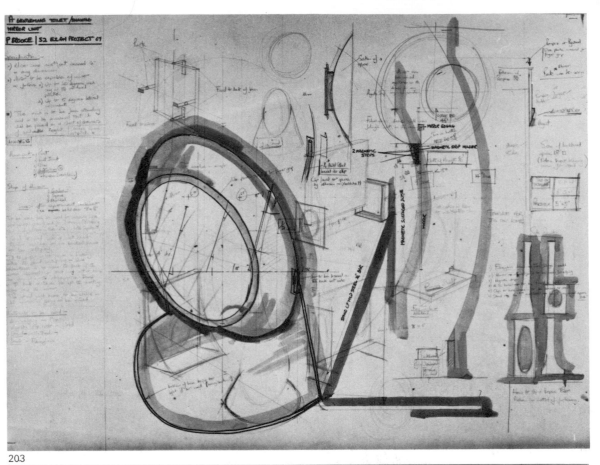
203

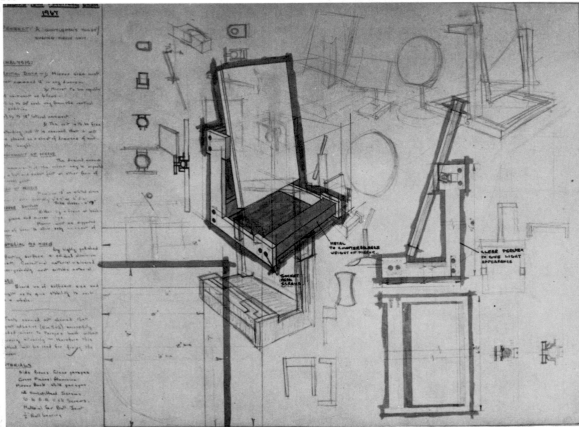
204

203–204 Design analysis sheets for toilet mirror.

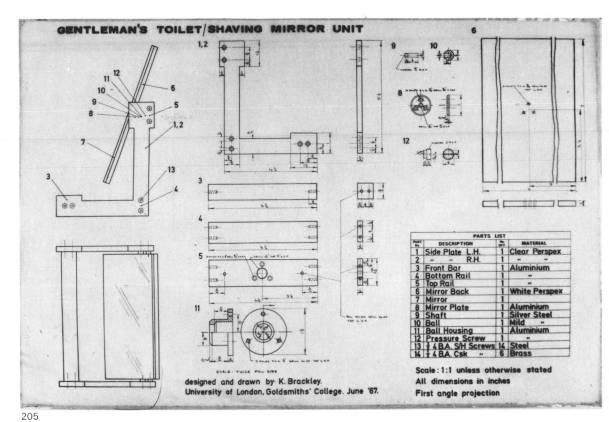

205 Working drawings.

205

206–12 Finished mirrors – the
variety of solutions is notable
(see overleaf).

206

119

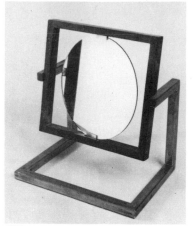

207

208

209

210

211

212

Case History 8

Eaton Hall College of Education, Retford

This case history is about an experimental design exercise carried out in a secondary school during a demonstration lesson. It is worth quoting in full from a report on the work prepared by Mr F O Zanker (Principal Lecturer at the College):

'For this experimental project eight boys were taken from the second-year A-stream of a secondary school. They were selected so that a wide range of general abilities was represented, but they did not have any particular flair for craftwork. Their craft background had consisted largely of the conventional approach and any reference to design had been associated with looking at and discussing pictures of products; they had not been involved in any previous experience of the design process. The only material with which they were familiar was wood, and their contact with it had taken the form of two half-periods per week over a period of four terms.

'It was decided to select a topic which would allow every boy, regardless of ability, to make a valid contribution. A programme of events, designed to lead to certain discoveries and eventually to a solution of the design problem, was worked out very carefully.

'The following points were considered as educational requirements:

1   Every boy should be guaranteed some degree of measurable success.
2   The topic for investigation had to contain –
    A centre of interest which would appeal to a boy at this age level.
    A process of elementary logic.
    An experience of new materials and their associated craft content.
    A conclusion which could be tested and assessed on its technical and visual merits.
    A conclusion which could be taken a stage further into other fields of experiment and discovery.
3   The use of wood as a material was considered desirable for the opening stages of the project for two reasons. Wood was a material with which the boys were familiar, but the main reason was to show that wood could be a means to other ends and not simply an end in itself. In this instance it happened to be the ideal material for carrying out design development work.

'The topic selected was to study the shape of a boat hull. In the introductory stages the aim was to examine possible developments and to establish an understanding of certain fundamental principles. It was significant that, although all the boys had at some time or other been on a boat, none could give really valid answers to such questions as:

Why does a boat float?
How is the weight of a boat measured?
What materials are used in boat building?
Why are boats shaped in a variety of shapes and forms?

These questions were answered through practical activities.

'*Why does a boat float?* A thin, deep-sided plastic saucer was placed on the surface of the water in the experiment tank, and its depth of penetration examined. The boys were now asked: 'If the depression made by the saucer in the surface of the water could be lifted out as a complete portion of water, what would its weight be equal to?' At this stage the boys were invited to place ballast in the saucer until it sat as low in the water as possible without sinking. It was very quickly established from this experiment that the saucer full of water, when weighed, was equal to the weight of the saucer and its ballast.

'It was thus established that *Displacement* = weight of boat. This is where the first real discovery was made by the boys which would influence their own ideas about hull design – they had discovered the importance of weight in relation to size and the resulting safe buoyancy margin, called *Freeboard*. The next question was – how do we consider a suitable shape to cater for this?

'*What governs the shape of a boat?* Various sections of wood were now placed in the tank by the boys. They quickly discovered that a piece of buoyant material will always float on its largest surface area unless some other factor is introduced in the form of a weight – a keel for example. Thin cut-outs of a variety of shapes representing the plan view of boats were now tested. Finger pressure was applied at a number of points on a given shape and the resistance and any instability discussed. Another design criteria was established – the importance of beam in the right place – *Lateral and longitudinal stability*.

121

'Each boy was now confronted with his first decision. He was given some thin card for making his own templates and also an easily shaped block of jelutong 7 by 2 by 1 in. The hull shape he was asked to produce had to fulfil the following requirements given in the form of a brief:

1 The hull had to float in a position so that the deck-line was horizontal to the water both laterally and longitudinally.
2 It had to be capable of passing through the water smoothly at a given speed.

'Any shaping tool which was convenient was used and it was soon apparent to the boys that they had to screw their blocks to small holding pieces for ease of handling. The eight shapes they produced proved to be extremely interesting from the following points of view:

No two were alike.

Round-bilge, hard-chine and flat bottoms were all considered, partly because these were sketched on the blackboard as possible sections, but more positively because each boy had the conviction that his shape was the right one for his boat.

'Constant testing during the shaping process needed no prompting, perhaps because boys (and teachers) love playing with water. Vaseline was applied to the shapes before placing in the water and the implications of removing timber from particular areas of the shapes were approached in a very thoughtful manner. Lively discussions took place, and the production of the shapes took precedence over the particular skills of tool manipulation – the actual standard of toolwork was, according to the boys, the best that they had ever produced. One boy remarked that he found a spokeshave easy to use on this occasion because he was so busy thinking about the shape of his boat that he didn't have time to think about the tool – it just seemed to work by itself.

'When all the hulls had been tested for their attitude on the water it was considered that, after all, in reality boats aren't just solid blocks and that these models presented very little freeboard because of their size/weight ratio. Because of this they had considerable resistance when pushed forward. The next question was how could the exact shape of the hulls be reproduced in a hollow form?...

'Comparison of the moulded shapes was now made – the sculptural effect of the plaster moulds, and the cured hull shapes taken from the moulds, caused considerable comment. The shapes in glass fibre gave the boys tremendous satisfaction when they compared their efforts alongside that of a traditional tug-boat which would not even float upright. The testing of the glass shapes took place alongside the original shapes in wood. The increase in freeboard was obvious, and slight change in the floating attitude in some cases could be seen.

'Each boy now had a hull made to his own design, and the opportunity of producing further hulls in glass fibre from the plaster moulds. Apart from this, a very demanding exercise had been experienced. What is more the work contained within it the origins of another cycle of activity (not yet complete) concerned with the means of propulsion for the hulls.'

213–219 These illustrations record the sequence of events in a demonstration lesson organized by F O Zanker, Principal Lecturer at Eaton Hall College of Education, Retford. The project, which involved eight boys in their second year at secondary school, was concerned with the principles involved in designing boat hulls. 213 The diagram shows the principles of displacement and freeboard which are fundamental to hull design and which were experienced in practical terms by the boys; 214 Shaping a wooden hull; 215 A wide variety of different designs were produced.

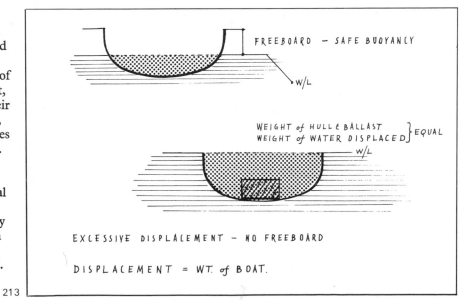

FREEBOARD – SAFE BUOYANCY

W/L

WEIGHT of HULL & BALLAST
WEIGHT of WATER DISPLACED } EQUAL

W/L

EXCESSIVE DISPLACEMENT – NO FREEBOARD

DISPLACEMENT = WT. of BOAT.

213

214

215

216

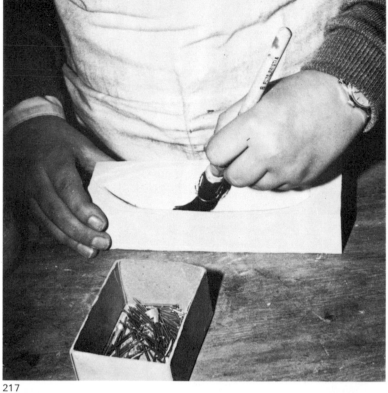

217

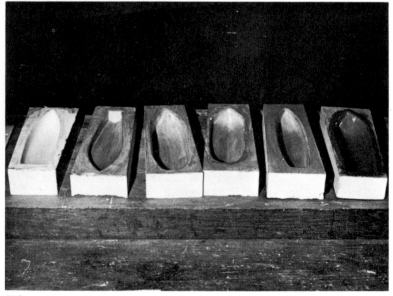

218

219

216 Testing the displacement of
wooden hulls in the water tank.
217–218 Plaster moulds were
made from the wooden originals.
These moulds were used as the
basis for versions of the hulls
made in glass fibre lamination.
219 Comparative testing between
a solid wood hull and a hollow
glass fibre hull of the same shape.

Organization and Resources

6 CONSUMER EDUCATION

PETER GOLDMAN C.B.E.

In this contribution Peter Goldman, Director and Secretary of the Consumers' Association, looks at the specific problems involved in consumer education and gives examples of successful solutions from Britain and the United States.

In many industrial societies consumer unions have now followed trade unions as instruments and agencies of reform. I do not mean by this that consumer unions have been modelled on trade unions; still less do I foresee their historical development taking a similar course. My point is simpler and more fundamental. Trade unions grew up because of the need to correct an intolerable disequilibrium in the economic system – the lack of balance between the power of capital and the power of labour. They provided a means by which workers through collective action could secure wages and conditions which no individual worker could obtain for himself. At a later stage of economic development consumer unions have been formed to redress another sharply felt lack of balance – that which exists between the power of the seller and the power of the buyer.

This lack of balance was highlighted in Britain in 1962 by the Molony Committee on consumer protection. 'The business of making and selling', said their official report, 'is highly organized, often in large units, and calls to its aid at every step complex and highly expert skills. The business of buying is conducted by the smallest unit, the individual consumer, relying on the guidance afforded by experience, if he possesses it and if not on instinctive but not always rational thought processes.'

It is important to add that the situation so described is not a static one. On the contrary, in the absence of institutional and educational checks, the imbalance between the strong seller and the weak buyer must inevitably worsen as economic development gathers pace. For the more technologically advanced a society becomes, and the larger the cornucopia of goods and services it produces, the less able are individual consumers to rely on experience or hunch. They may enjoy the blessings of affluence and free choice; but they will still be faced with unfamiliar merchandise, often of great technical complexity – goods whose quality they cannot judge by inspection, whose packaging may be deceptive, whose advertisers may fasten on superficial or irrelevant charms, and whose retail distributors in an age of self-service are increasingly unable or unwilling to give guidance.

The problem has been created and magnified within a single lifetime. Fifty years ago our grandmothers knew, with inflexible certainty, that ordinary soda and plain carbolic soap were the best washing agents they could purchase. But now, a dozen different dazzling detergents, each with its own gimmicky claims, compete noisily for custom. As a result, sure knowledge is replaced by nagging doubt. Which of them really gets things cleanest and gives best value for money?

With something as inexpensive and regularly used as a washing powder or liquid, conscientious housewives might at least attempt to answer that question unscientifically, each for herself, by trying them all. But to do the same with thirty different kinds of refrigerator, or fifty different models of fog lamp, or 100 different makes of strawberry jam, or 200 different brands of mechanical contraceptive, would require a consumer with quite unusual financial or physical resources. This was the very practical origin of consumer unions. Just as workers had been organized to achieve collectively what they could never have won individually, so increasing numbers of consumers decided to pool their resources in consumer testing associations to find out collectively what they could never have discovered by themselves.

220 Consumer education can be an aspect of many different activities. Mathematics problems can easily be given a consumer orientation and so can science. In an even more direct sense housecraft practical work brings young people into critical contact with a whole range of domestic products. Girls quickly notice and remember which cookers are difficult to clean, which snag their stockings and which utensils are too heavy or too easily dented.

220

221–222 Pages from a Certificate of Secondary Education (C.S.E.) examination notebook on furnishing a house produced by a girl in a Leicestershire school. Such studies help young people prepare for the pressures of advertising and salesmanship in adult life (see also p.128).

221

This essentially educational movement began in the most advanced industrial society, the U.S.A., more than a generation ago. In 1927 an economist and an electrical engineer, both of high standing and repute, wrote a book called *Your Money's Worth*. In compelling detail the authors pointed out: that the United States Government was itself a major purchaser of consumer goods; that it used its own agencies such as the National Bureau of Standards to test the quality of those goods; and that by choosing on the basis of these tests the best value for money, it saved itself 100 million dollars a year – or 30% of its total relevant expenditure. If, asked the authors, the government of the United States had such facilities to become a discriminating consumer, why should not similar facilities be available to the citizens of the United States.

The answer was dramatic. *Your Money's Worth* quickly became both a best seller and the book most frequently stolen from public libraries. One of its authors organized a consumers' club in New York out of which grew the independent testing organization known as Consumers' Research Inc. (C.R.). In 1935 C.R. split, and the break-away organization – Consumers' Union of U.S. Inc. (C.U.) – was later to go from strength to strength. Today C.U. is still by far the largest consumer union in the world, with an annual income of over eight million dollars, its own excellent and extensive laboratories, and circulation for its test-based *Consumer Reports* of one and a half million. But the same forces that brought consumer organizations into existence in America have, since World War II, spread to many other parts of the industrialized world. The International Organization of Consumers Unions (I.O.C.U.), which was founded in 1960, now has forty-four members and affiliates coming from twenty-seven different countries and every continent. All of these are honestly dedicated to a consumer educational effort, and most of the larger members regularly undertake comparative testing and publish the results of such tests, including brand names and prices, in their magazines and bulletins.

The members of I.O.C.U. differ significantly in structure, methods and attitudes; and these differences often reflect national characteristics and politics to an uncanny degree. But all the testing organizations have certain basic features in common. They are all non-profit making. They are all independent of industrial and business influences. None of them accepts advertisements in its publications. And none of them permits commercial exploitation of its test results and recommendations.

The practical and psychological importance of these characteristics cannot be over-emphasized. In the modern world, with its sophisticated methods of communication, there are many sources of consumer information or misinformation. There is advertising by brand-owners and by retailers. There are the specialized columns of the press and the magazine programmes of radio and television. There is such guidance as can still be offered by shop-keepers and shop assistants. There are quality seals and informative labels. There is even the advice tendered by your colleagues, your friends and your mother-in-law. But amid all this bewildering variety of contradictory and partial information, only the consumer testing organizations satisfy the need for full technical evidence by witnesses who emphatically serve no interest whatsoever except that of the ultimate consumer himself.

When the British Consumers' Association (C.A.) began its work in 1957, the first print order for its magazine *Which?* was 5000. By its twelfth anniversary it had a subscribing membership of over 600,000. It had won the qualified but powerful commendation of the Molony Committee which declared that 'where faults of design, quality and sometimes safety have come to light, the reports have served to draw them imperatively to the manufacturer's attention'. And it had received messages of congratulation and encouragement from the leaders of all three political parties who vouched, to quote the Prime Minister, that: 'An aware and informed buying public is the best stimulus to the raising of standards by manufacturers and traders generally.'

But (leaving aside the attacks of certain sensitive manufacturers whose products had at one time or another received unfavourable notice) two friendly, constructive and persistent criticisms were also raised – both of them central to the subject of this book. The first criticism was elegantly expressed by a leader in the October 1967 issue of *Design* which said: 'What matters to C.A. is whether a product works, is well made, reliable, easy to repair and good value for money. This assumes that people have a clinical, scientific approach to shopping – but in fact, this is not so. Time and time again people will put up with inconvenient and unreliable products just because they like them. Cars, radios, prams, washing machines all these things are bought for many reasons besides the mechanical ones, yet these other reasons have been largely ignored by C.A. Instead of reinforcing the celebrated dictum, "form follows function", C.A. has, if anything, suggested that function is all that matters,

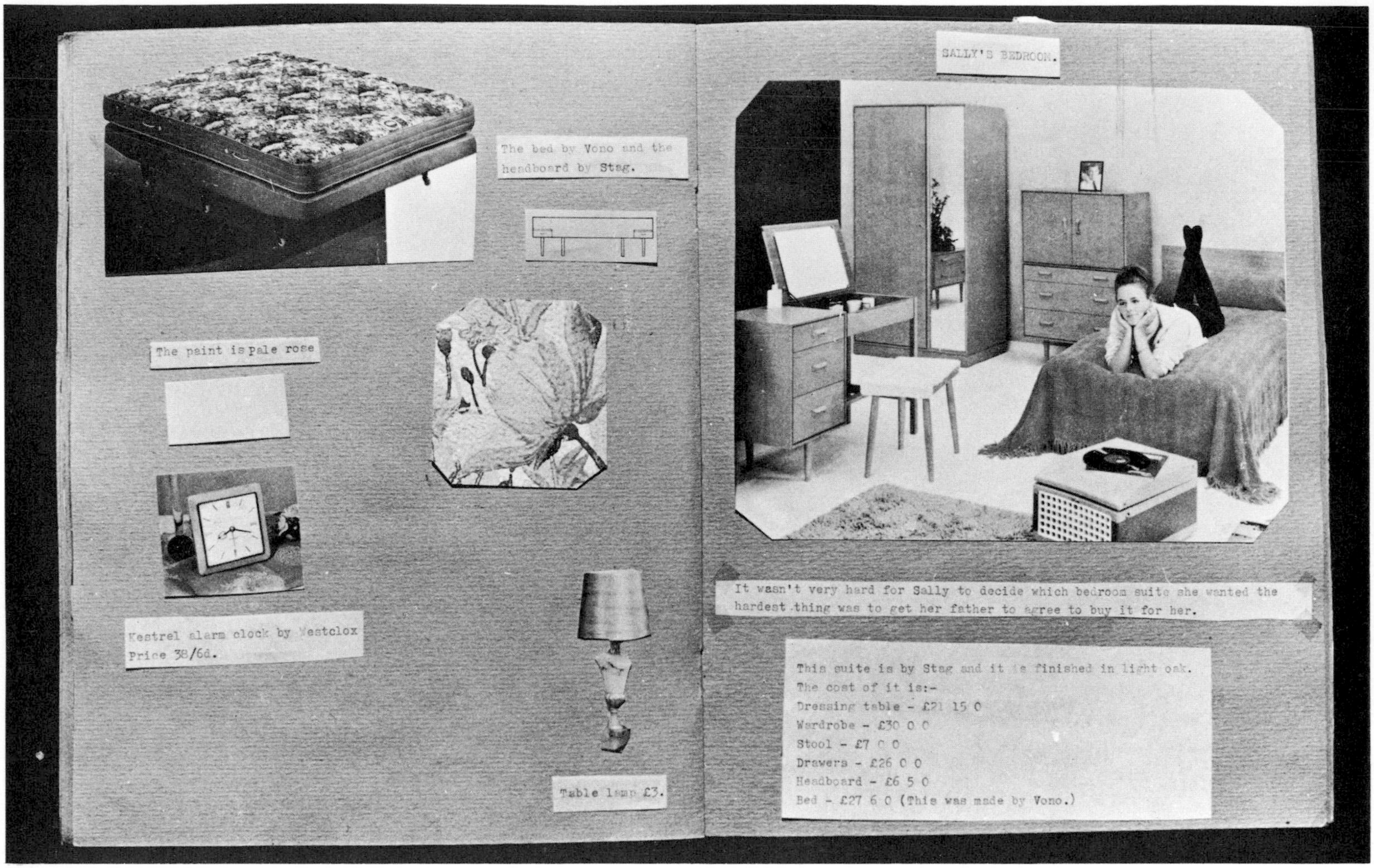
SALLY'S BEDROOM.
The bed by Vono and the headboard by Stag.
The paint is pale rose
Kestrel alarm clock by Westclox
Price 38/6d.
Table lamp £3.
It wasn't very hard for Sally to decide which bedroom suite she wanted the hardest thing was to get her father to agree to buy it for her.
This suite is by Stag and it is finished in light oak.
The cost of it is:-
Dressing table - £21 15 0
Wardrobe - £30 0 0
Stool - £7 0 0
Drawers - £26 0 0
Headboard - £6 5 0
Bed - £27 6 0 (This was made by Vono.)

222

222 Pages from a C.S.E. examination notebook.

even when form heads madly in the opposite direction. But a product's shape, colour and visual effect on its environment is as important as its mechanical efficiency.'

It is, of course, true that the Molony Committee went off the rails in asserting that they could not view design as 'a primary consumer interest'. C.A. certainly does not take its own cue from this assertion. What it does say (more sensibly and more modestly) is that unlike the Council of Industrial Design it is not itself an authoritative judge of whether a product is beautiful or ugly. Its magazine *Which?* gives photographs of many of the products on which it is reporting to help people exercise their own aesthetic judgement, and it shows the CoID symbol against any tested product on the Design Index to enable people to lean on the council's judgement if they wish. What it also says (and insists upon not through philistinism but sheer common sense) is that no design, however sensuously pleasing, is good unless it is efficient. In fact, in the early days, as the editor of *Which?* pointed out in the Penguin Survey *Business & Industry 1967*, 'Some of the comparative testing organizations' reports showed a few of the council's favourites behaving badly in practice. So the CoID started a system of liaison with testing organizations – including the consumers' testing organizations – whereby they were told of any of the products which failed in a test (and could withdraw it from the Index if they wanted to), and whereby they attach references to test reports on goods appearing in the Index.' In these ways the two organizations do derive some nourishment from one another, and the individual consumer is helped to strike his or her personal balance between sense and sensibility.

A second important criticism of C.A. relates to the socially unrepresentative nature of its membership. Barely one-third belong to the lower middle and skilled working classes, and only a tiny percentage to the manual working classes. The typical reader of *Which?* is sophisticated, urbanized, well educated and fairly affluent. In this respect C.A. is certainly no worse though equally no better than any other consumer organization. Their magazines, like ours, are unacceptable to whole sections of the population because they require efforts of critical concentration which these people are neither educated nor willing to give.

Time, no doubt, is on our side, for, as education increases both in quality and quantity, so will our potential readership. But here and now, and for a long time to come, we are faced with a very relevant question of social justice. It simply is not good enough, as the Molony Committee seemed to think, to consign comparative test information to the safe keeping of the educationally privileged ('we are as conscious of the dangers as of the advantages of disseminating them – in present or in simplified form – to consumers of lesser wisdom'). For it is precisely the educationally under-privileged who are most vulnerable to misinformation, least able to afford expensive mistakes and therefore in greatest need of independent assessments and guidance. But how are we to find a way of presenting this information to them?

The answer, I believe, lies in the highly successful advisory centres or 'consumer clinics' which have been developed in certain central European cities – most notably in Vienna. There the Austrian consumer organization's own testing and research staff, together with independent experts in the physical and domestic sciences, industrial design, economics and law, form a corps of highly trained personal advisers. They take it in turns to be available for consultation in the afternoon and evening of most weekdays and every Saturday. And they are available at the time and in the place where most of the relevant shopping decisions are taken, since their advisory centre is superbly located, plumb in the middle of Vienna's equivalent of Oxford Street. The verbal advice they give there can be hand-tailored to the circumstances and requirements of individual shoppers. It can get things clear by argument and counter-argument. Above all, it can be demonstrated: for the advisory centre's showrooms can house exhibitions of the competing brands of major consumer durables. In this way purchasers are able to examine both the design *and* the test ratings of the available products in conditions free from sales pressure. The whole enterprise – now attracting 250,000 inquirers yearly – represents an achievement in consumer education for adults which, given the support of public finance, could and should be widely emulated here.

But what about consumer education for children? This has been a late starter; but in many of the countries in which I.O.C.U. members are most active, serious thought is now given to educating the consumers of the next generation in schools and colleges. The Molony Committee very cautiously observed that there might be a place in British school education for some attention to consumer affairs. But, aware of the dangers of overloading formal school curricula, they burked any attempts to define this place. The Newsom Committee on secondary education were rather more definite about the way in which consumer questions could increase the relevance to life of what was taught in school.

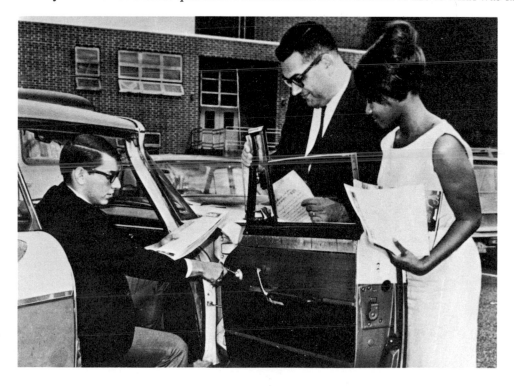

223 Students at the Lincoln High School, Yonkers, New York, taking part in a consumer education programme which takes motor-cars as its central theme. (Courtesy: Westchester Rockland Newspaper Group, White Plains, N.Y.)

224

224 Study sheet comparing types of toys prepared as part of the sixth-form liberal studies course at the Cavendish Grammar School.

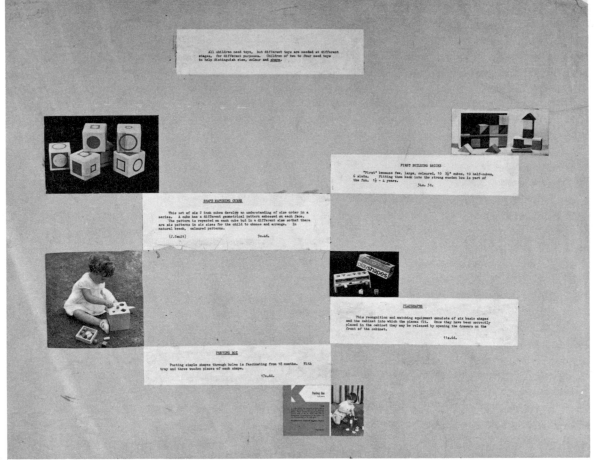

224

They were notably forthright about the need to strengthen children's critical powers and to overcome 'their inability to see when they are being got at, particularly through some modern sales methods'. On the other hand, they wisely observed how wrong it would be to leave pupils with the idea that criticism is intrinsically negative: 'A sound, positive judgement must start with valuing properly the good things they enjoy'.

That the Reports of these two Committees, with quite different terms of reference, should have intersected on this issue exemplified the growing conviction that consumer education was important. But as the Research Institute for Consumer Affairs (R.I.C.A.) noted in 1964, 'this conviction co-exists with considerable uncertainty about what consumer education actually *is*'. So R.I.C.A. (a sister-organization of C.A.) set itself, in a symposium published that year on *Consumer Education – conceptions and resources*, to study both scope and context in depth. It came up with the conclusion that consumer education should not be a new subject in the school curriculum. Rather, 'it comprises education in certain specific skills (e.g. home furnishing) and aptitudes (e.g. an understanding of design) which are relevant to being a contented and efficient consumer; it can also be integrated into curricular subjects (e.g. consumer problems can provide examples for lessons in arithmetic); it overlaps with large sections of general education for citizenship (e.g. consumer legislation); and it can be a dimension for all education, balancing use values against production values.'

How such ideas may be translated into practical and enjoyable lessons can best be seen from the wide-ranging experiment that has taken place recently at Lincoln High School in Yonkers, New York. There in the spring of 1964 – because of the interest shown by students, teachers and some parents – three important developments occurred. First, teachers in seven different departments and the two principals organized the school's Consumer Education Committee. Second, the committee planned and conducted a series of special assemblies on consumer topics attended by the entire student body. Thirdly, each teacher on his own initiative introduced consumer-orientated units, projects, or emphases into the courses.

The first (and most frequently repeated) of the special assemblies was on the subject of automobiles. For this programme, a panel, including a local insurance agent, a used-car dealer, an eminent lawyer, an automotive engineer from Consumers' Union, together with student leaders, held a lively discussion on the purchase and upkeep of a car. According to the social-studies teacher who co-ordinated this enterprise, 'The rapt attention of the students during the programme, the content of their questions, and their comments afterwards – all showed the attractiveness and value of this all-school educational experience'. Afterwards the used-car dealer who had participated in the assembly parked one of his cars in the school lot. While the boys from the industrial arts classes watched, C.U.'s automotive engineer pointed out the good and bad features of the car under study, and demonstrated some of the on-the-lot car tests that a consumer himself could apply in deciding whether to buy.

Though all the assemblies have clearly had their value – and one enthusiastic student described them as 'one of the smartest ideas ever introduced in any school system' – Lincoln's chief success has undoubtedly been in incorporating consumer education material into established, traditional courses. In English classes, for example, students are made aware of the part language plays in influencing their behaviour and are then set to analyse the assertions made in advertisements and television commercials. In social-studies classes, emphasis is placed on consumer legislation and the part played by various government agencies in consumer protection. In economics courses, pupils are encouraged to apply basic principles by budgeting their allowances or earnings realistically. In science classes, the chemistry of neutralization is linked with popularly advertised remedies for indigestion, the absorption and use of water in the human body is related to constipation remedies, and so on. In the mathematics classroom teachers analyse what makes up the cost of goods to the consumer, and how to compute the true rate of interest on savings, investments and loans. In the business course, students are taught to approach each problem first from the producer's point of view, then from the consumer's point of view and last from the interrelated point of view of producer and consumer. In home economics, there are lessons on the art of spending – how to select carefully, buy wisely and manage personal and family finances.

In the industrial arts department, to quote its director, 'We endeavour to help students to develop a sense of aesthetic values – that is, an appreciation of good design and workmanship. In the field of product design, students are led to distinguish between the bizarre features that prevail for a time and the simple, adaptable, well-proportioned and harmonious features that persist over the years.

225 The cover of *Which? in Secondary Schools,* published by the Consumers' Association and containing school exercises based on *Which?* reports.

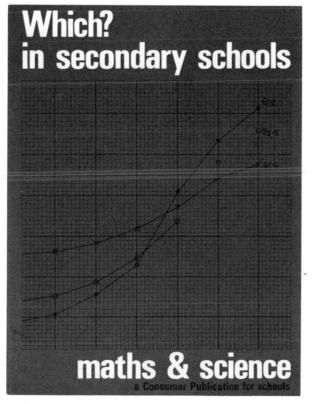

225

Students are, moreover, taught to be discriminating in the selection and use of what they may purchase; they learn about many commonly used things – products that vary considerably in kind, cost, and durability. They are aided in building thoughtful attitudes – attitudes that help them avoid waste and secure the greatest possible satisfaction and service from what they have. In addition, students are assisted and encouraged to make sound judgements – judgements that are based upon comparisons. Such comparisons, of course, require a consideration of the qualities, that, when combined, yield overall ratings: 'Excellent', 'Good', 'Fair', 'Poor', or 'Not Acceptable'. To cite one example – an article of household furniture – students learn to judge its craftsmanship as superior or inferior; and other qualities, such as appearance, construction, artistic merit, usefulness, adaptability, style and finish. In this way, they learn to evaluate the article as a whole.'

The success of the Lincoln High School experiment owes much to Consumers' Union (to which I referred earlier as the front-runner among consumer testing organizations); for C.U. responded to a request for help in this venture and made its educational director available as a consultant. In Britain, almost from the first issue of *Which?*, Consumers' Association too has been caught up with the educational world. It responded to the keen interest expressed in its work by providing special discounts when its magazine was bought for educational purposes, and by creating a speakers' panel which still (despite the growing diversity of its audiences) addresses appreciative groups in schools and colleges at the rate of one a week. From the panel's reports and from individual teachers it soon became clear that *Which?* was being used in the classroom – especially for teaching English and housecraft, but also in such varied contexts as French at primary level and the studies of post-graduate sociologists.

Although *Which?* is not conceived as a teaching aid, the initiative and imagination of those who were using it as a text-book have encouraged C.A. to produce consumer-orientated teaching material for some aspects of the school curriculum. The first fruit appeared in 1967 with the publication of *Which? in Secondary Schools: Maths & Science*. This is based on twenty-five reprinted *Which?* reports – from nylon stockings and boys' blazers to cars in action – and contains exercises (with answers) and class practicals prepared with the help of a group of lecturers from Goldsmiths' College, London. The book is an experiment and will in due course be followed up by an investigation into how it has been used in a selection of schools and what its likely effects will be on tomorrow's consumer.

But certainly its approach – the inclusion of a consumer *emphasis* in many subjects of the curriculum – is one that has proved most successful in the United States and has the official blessing of the British Consumer Council. It is this approach which puts consumer education and design education so much on the same footing. For, as the deputy director of CoID wrote in the R.I.C.A. study already quoted: 'School programmes are already so full that it would be difficult to inject design appreciation as a subject into these time-tables which are already overcrowded. It must rather become an attitude which colours all the subjects and activities.' And the reason why these interlinked subjects of design appreciation and consumer orientation require to colour and liberalize the curriculum was well expressed by the then research director of R.I.C.A. in that same study. 'Everyone', he wrote, 'is, directly or indirectly, a producer, and everyone is a consumer. These are not opposing classes in society (though there may obviously be conflicts between some producers and some consumers); they are dual roles played by all individuals. Much education – from basic literacy to the development of sensibility through art and literature – affects the performance of these two roles but clearly transcends them. Even though we are all producers and consumers, our education as consumers has been neglected, whereas our education as producers has become more dominant and acquired more prestige: all vocational education is dedicated to it, whether in book-keeping, engineering, or theology, and much so-called general education in schools and universities is in fact a preparation for work (i.e. production). So education reflects and reinforces those distorted social values which subordinate people to the system and which are at odds with some of the simplest facts about ourselves – that we take as well as give, spend money as well as make it, and have lives to lead that are not confined by the time-sheet.' Thus consumer education in common with design education serves to redress an important human balance.

Organization and Resources

7 COUNCIL OF INDUSTRIAL DESIGN

SYDNEY FOOTT

Right from its inception the Council of Industrial Design has been involved in educational activities of various kinds. In this contribution Miss Sydney Foott, the council's Education Officer, describes the services available and the way in which they have developed over the years.

It is frequently said that the activities of the Council of Industrial Design are educational, and in a sense this is true. Its aim is to encourage people to look critically at the things which surround them, and in this way to bring out their own latent talents. Initially the Council's activities were largely educational in the more formal sense – World War II and the early days of peace gave people a taste and an opportunity for learning. They were less self-conscious about 'culture' then, and films, filmstrips and wall-charts had a moral lesson. In the first four or five years the CoID produced a number of visual aids of various types – wall-charts, films, filmstrips and design folios. Much of this material followed closely on the forms devised in the war, particularly by the Army Bureau of Current Affairs. It included a series of filmstrips, mainly on furniture, wall-charts on furniture, an illustrated design quiz and a film coyly entitled *Designing Women*. None of this material was produced in response to a specific demand – at that stage.

The education section was an early part of the CoID and the first education officer was Robin Darwin (now Sir Robin Darwin, Vice-Chancellor of the Royal College of Art), who was at the CoID in 1946. During this time he produced a paper on art education which has had a far reaching effect on teaching in this country.

Design Folios: after considerable discussion with the Ministry of Education, and advice from many educationists, the council in 1948 produced a teaching aid which broke new ground – Design Folios. Each folio consisted of twelve photographs (14 in. by 17 in.) briefly captioned – so briefly indeed that sometimes the caption was as terse as 'Bath mat'. These twelve photographs were accompanied by a critical essay and a set of captions, as well as reading list, films and filmstrips and list of further activities in and out of school. Each set dealt with one particular material or subject and, at least in the initial stages, the captions were kept to a minimum. Titles included Teapots and Boats and Chairs. A certain amount was done to find out how schools responded to the material.

L.C.C. Experiment: also experimental was the work undertaken at the instigation of and financed by the London County Council. Here the CoID devised and designed a display of materials for use in schools. Each set of four display boxes showed the material or materials, the methods by which it is manufactured, and some products. The materials included clay, wood, paper, metal and glass. They were sent to schools selected by the L.C.C. art inspectorate and remained in each school for a term at a time.

Originally it was thought there should be a minimum number of captions, but after experience in the schools it was decided to issue a comprehensive catalogue, which also offered a book list and suggested further activities such as making a collection of similar objects, looking for historical examples, and seeing practising craftsmen at work. In addition, seven key objects were chosen in each box and these were referred to in drawings at the base in shallow, pull-out shelves. On each shelf was an extended caption, giving interesting design points. Although this was termed the L.C.C. 'experiment' much of its success was predetermined by the selection of suitable schools. It was clear, however, that

226

226 Right from its inception the Council of Industrial Design has been concerned with design education at secondary-school level. Shown here is a class using as a teaching aid one of the design folios which the CoID produced in its early days.

the displays had a great attraction for boys and girls, and often encouraged them to follow up design points. Selected schools included grammar, comprehensive and secondary modern. The displays appeared to be of equal interest to boys and girls, although the latter were perhaps slightly less interested.

In response to the children's demands two sets of blank boxes were provided, in which the schools were free to devise and mount their own exhibitions. These met with varying success – usually little was done until the end of the term, but occasionally interesting displays were mounted, both of craft work and of prized possessions from home: plaster alsatian dogs, dancing ladies, seashells, or ephemera such as containers. Eventually the administration of the scheme was passed over to the L.C.C. (now the I.L.E.A.) where it now comes within their general school loans scheme. Advice on museum and school loan services covering contemporary products has been given in a number of other cases, but never again on the scale of the L.C.C. experiment.

The Design Centre: from its opening in 1956, groups of school children and young adults have visited the Design Centre, frequently by appointment. Groups coming to the Design Centre vary considerably in age and attainment, from 17-to 18-year old sixth-formers down to the eager 11-year olds, from secondary schools and grammar schools, from London and as far away as Hull or Belfast. Some children are physically or mentally handicapped – blind and partially-sighted, deaf, physically handicapped, educationally subnormal. It is moving to see the interest with which the blind and partially-sighted 'look' at objects. Each group of four or five is accompanied by a receptionist or by the education officer, and the children are fascinated by shapes and textures – the most popular object with the boys being the motor-bicycle.

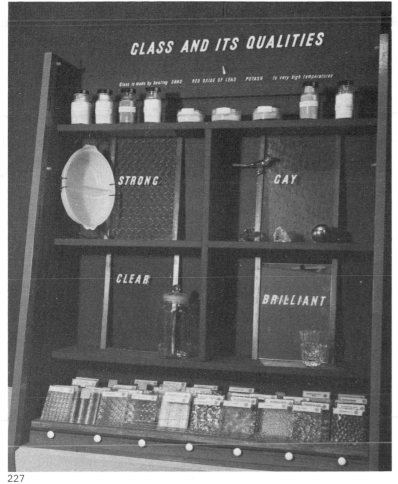

227

228

227–230 The London County
Council asked the CoID to
prepare a series of experimental
exhibitions which would be sent
to selected schools in box form.
Shown here are two of the
original displays and boxes used
by schools to mount their own
exhibitions.

229

230

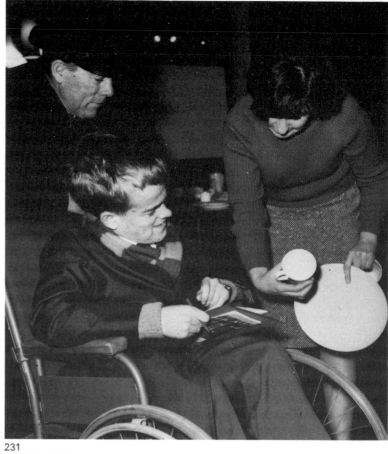

231

232

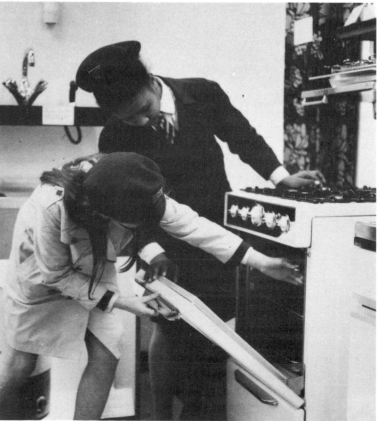

233

230 Box exhibition for LCC
schools. The example shown
here has been used by children
to display their own work.

231 A physically handicapped
boy on a visit to the Design
Centre.

Educationally subnormal groups are always deeply interested and well behaved; great care must be taken to see that the children fully understand in advance what is happening and that they feel able to undertake the tasks set. A specially simple design quiz is available, and it is always read over to them first for the benefit of the less literate. These children have a great sense of responsibility and, as with the physically handicapped, look after the less able members.

Sixth-formers are often surprisingly ignorant of the world of design, and although they are well informed on science and the space race they know little or nothing of modern buildings or furniture or the cities in which they live. But it is the school-leavers to whom the centre seems most appealing. After all, they will soon be earning and soon after that setting up home. They have seldom had the opportunity of this glorified window shopping – in their local stores one cannot often browse about without being asked to buy, and it is a change for them to be able to seek information without strings attached. It is for this type of boy and girl – perhaps more particularly the girls in this predominantly domestic setting – that the design quiz forms are intended. Where possible groups are given an introductory talk in the conference room, with carpet, comfortable chairs and a welcome. They are invited to give their ideas as to priorities in buying, and to discuss the content of the talk. Only too often the teacher offers answers – sometimes one supposes because he is conscious of the fact that the children have not been taught anything on these lines; at other times because it is indeed new and exciting to himself. The quiz forms are couched in simple language, asking questions on function, quality and appearance, and they suggest that answers should be drawn, not written. The answers vary considerably, but if the questions have made the children look more closely, then they have at least done something.

Many schools plan their visits to the Design Centre admirably, and these obviously form part of the children's general design education. They are part of a pattern – perhaps a highlight, but something which is a continuous process. For these the quiz is often superfluous – they already have their objectives and follow them out.

With other schools the visit may be a conscious attempt to include design education, but with little or no advance preparation. For these schools *Notes for School Visits* are provided. This lists on the front all the necessary administrative detail, and the back of the form suggests activities before, during and after the visit. As with all material concerned with a creative process such as design it is unwise to be dogmatic. Projects which succeed with one group are a failure with another. By suggesting a variety of possible approaches it is hoped that inexperienced teachers may be encouraged to try out a variety of methods.

The objections to the earlier Design Folios were that they were too static in their approach, and

232–234 The Design Centre has
special facilities for school
parties and welcomes such visits.

234

1 USE AND FUNCTION

Often the simplest things are the most useful. Find something in The Centre which is really simple and easy to use, which would be used in the home every day.

cup. Rife, fork.

Special jobs often need special tools or products. Find something in The Centre which would be used only occasionally, but which would need a product planned for that particular function.

£32•16

NO reference numbers please. Draw a picture of the product in the space provided (or write a short description) and give the price. Colour it in if desired.

2 QUALITY

Quality depends partly on the material, partly on the workmanship. Quality can help improve function, strength and appearance. The best quality is seldom cheap, but good quality need not necessarily be expensive. This is where one must decide how much one can afford to pay.

Find two cups and saucers, one made of earthenware, one of bone china. Could you tell the difference just by looking at them?

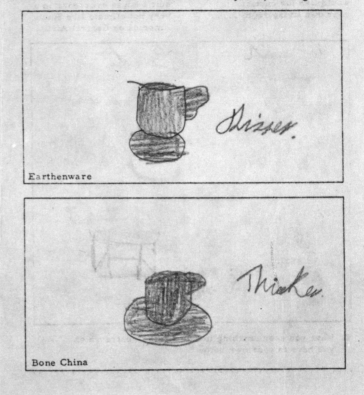

Earthenware

Bone China

235–238 Quiz forms supplied by the CoID for schoolchildren to fill in when visiting the Design Centre.

tended to make all design teaching the same. Each teacher has something personal to contribute, and this can best be done by a series of experiments. Expensive equipment can tend to canalize teaching where it should be fluid and unconfined.

The council has recently started courses for teachers of teachers, believing that this is an effective means of disposing its comparatively small resources in the educational world. Colleges of education are invited to send their lecturers to a four-day course in the Design Centre. These courses started with one for art training centres, but their scope and contents are now being widened after consultation with colleges and institutes of education and it is hoped they will become a regular part of the Council's programme.

Educational work in Industry and the Retail Trade: apart from the work of the Education Section, the council undertakes courses in a variety of fields. Education in design is carried out within the council's Industrial Division – mainly in the engineering industries, but also by means of organised design tours overseas and conferences for manufacturers and designers of consumer goods. Since 1960, when a pilot course was organized for junior engineering staff for Hoovers, courses have been run twice-yearly for engineering staff, and latterly separate courses for engineering executives. These courses are intended in the first place to help draughtsmen and engineers to understand industrial design. There are also courses in design management for senior executives.

As well as the council's work with industry the Retail Section has, for seventeen years, organized courses for retail staff (mainly residential) in aspects of selling related to design, and is now planning

1 USE AND FUNCTION

Often the simplest things are the most useful. Find something in The Centre which is really simple and easy to use, which would be used in the home every day.

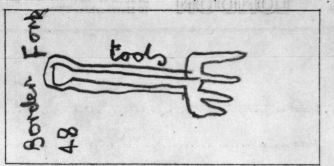

Special jobs often need special tools or products. Find something in The Centre which would be used only occasionally, but which would need a product planned for that particular function.

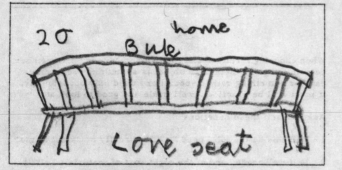

NO reference numbers please. Draw a picture of the product in the space provided (or write a short description) and give the price. Colour it in if desired.

236

3 APPEARANCE

As you go round The Design Centre, you will see some things which are familiar and others which are strange to you. People come here from all over the world, and obviously they have different needs and different tastes. The things which might not suit your home might be just right for someone else.

Choose one fabric which you would like for curtains in your own living room . . . . .

. . . . and one which would suit a house overseas, in a very hot climate like South America or Central Africa

4 Have you seen anything in The Design Centre which you have in your own home?

. . . .

237

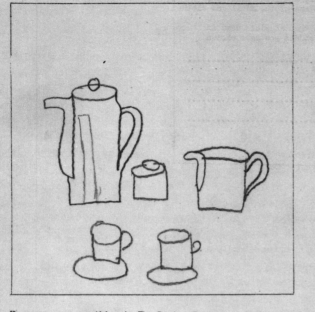

NICE TO LOOK AT
_____

Draw the teapot or coffeepot you have found in The Design
Centre which you like best.

Have you seen anything in The Design Centre you have
in your own home?
............High..Level..Radiant
............Fire.........................

238

238 An example from one of the
special forms supplied for
mentally handicapped children.

Lavender Hill
Secondary Modern school
Amies street
S.W.11
15th November 1961

Dear Miss Foot
        When I went to the design centre
on the 14th November, It was
very Interesting to see the
different equipment & Furniture
that are made in my own
country. I learnt that English
designs are more interesting and they
had more colour than other
countries would have on their
crockery or Toys. I like the
Kitchen equipment because some
of the equipment seemed to be
unusual. The Curtaining seemed
to be very colourful too. I enjoyed
it So much that when I got
home that night I could not
stop talking. Yours Faithfully
        I. Burton.

239

239 Letter thanking the CoID
education officer after a school
visit.
240 Discussion period in a course
for lecturers from colleges of
education held at the Design
Centre in January 1968.

240

some twenty each year. Initially these courses were intended for all staff, and covered furniture and furnishing fabrics, pottery and glass and other consumer goods. More recently they have been divided into courses for more junior staff and for buyers and managers, and this has proved an important step. Design is the responsibility of top management, and the interest and support of buyers are crucial in the field of design.

Another important – though less formal – link in design education has been provincial exhibitions. Local stores have, with the Council's co-operation, staged large-scale exhibitions often called *The Design Centre comes to* ... The display has been carried out to the same standard as the London Design Centre and school visits and talks for local teachers have been arranged by the Education Section. In this way children who are too far away to visit London can get an idea of what modern British goods are currently available and how wide a choice of well-designed things there can be.

A further extension of retail work has involved staff-training in stores. This is always carried out before a *Design Centre comes to* ... operation, so that the staff may make a reasonable response to public interest. This has a commercial side too, in that they are far more likely to sell the well-designed things in the display if they themselves are convinced of their merits.

Council Services: many of the council's services are educational, although by no means all come under the Education Section. *Design* magazine plays an influential part. It is read in a wide variety of schools and educational establishments, and the specially reduced rate for students has been a great success. Articles in the magazine dealing directly with educational subjects frequently arouse public discussion. Although *Design* magazine is primarily written for industry and commerce it is also widely read by educationists.

Slide and photographic libraries provide a valuable service both for the press and for educationists. The slides in particular are useful in projecting the CoID's image outside London and are widely used by lecturers and in schools and colleges.

The council's panel of lecturers consists of people qualified to speak on design – many of them teachers or designers who are available (at a fee!) in response to requests. The value of the one-off lecture – the afternoon or evening monthly meeting – is doubtful. Often the time might be better spent in showing a film or visiting an exhibition, and then discussing it. Far better are the planned programmes, where one speaker, or a series of lecturers, develops a theme. Even more useful (though rare except in adult education colleges) is the use of the residential weekend course.

Design Calendar, a monthly duplicated circular, indicates exhibitions, courses, conferences and films currently available in London and the provinces. It is issued without charge on request and keeps provincial readers in touch with design happenings.

The Education Section also produces a catalogue of some 500 recommended films and filmstrips, showing running-time and source of supply and giving a brief critical commentary. Additions to the film list are periodically listed in *Design Calendar*.

Careers in Design: the growth of interest in recent years in careers in industrial design is astonishing. Every day the council receives three or four enquiries about training, qualifications and prospects, and the educational qualifications of prospective designers grow steadily better. A leaflet on careers is available, and a booklet has now also been produced. More and more boys and girls with good A-levels in physics and mathematics are choosing to do their Diploma in Art and Design (Dip.A.D.) rather than a university course.

The Education Section also receives a large number of requests for help – for projects for C.S.E., background material on G.C.E., information for students' theses and general information for teachers. Requests range from information on table mats for a boys' school ('boys upset everything, from marmalade to fried egg') to impassioned requests for help from overseas students anxious to further their studies in England '. . . your message is really genuine to me – I pray for God's guidance in the industrial work'. There is an increasing number of requests from children doing C.S.E. work, often vaguely talking about 'a project on design', and these are met by a standard letter referring the writer to his own local resources. Such resources are not always exploited as much as they should be.

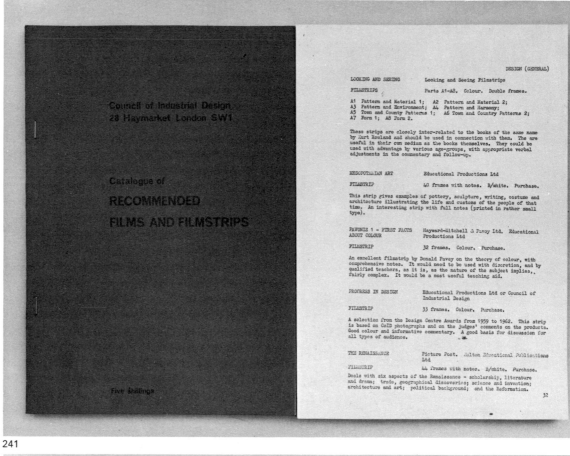

241 The catalogue of
Recommended Films and Filmstrips
published by the Council of
Industrial Design.

241

Furniture for the primary school

by Gillian Nayler

Last June, the new Eveline Lowe primary school opened in Camberwell. Here, on a bombed site off the Old Kent Road, 320 children between the ages of three and a half and nine are provided with what is probably the most stimulating environment for education this country can offer. For the building and its equipment are designed to demonstrate the ideal of progressive educationists that "the whole school must be a teaching instrument."

In the Eveline Lowe school, no two rooms are alike, and there are none of the conventional divisions between classroom and classroom, classroom and corridor, indoors and out. The school is designed as a unit to encourage the intermingling of age groups and the sharing of teaching: within the various areas into which the school has been subdivided, children are learning to read, write and count; they paint, cook and sew; they make pots, listen to stories and act; they run a shop and carry out scientific experiments. They are rarely all doing the same thing at the same time, and the school has been equipped with a special range of furniture designed to accommodate and stimulate all these activities.

The furniture for the Eveline Lowe school, like the school itself, was designed by the architects' development group at the Department of Education and Science (DES) in collaboration with the Inner London Education Authority (ILEA) design group and the Greater London Council (GLC) supplies division. The furniture consists of tables in four heights (17, 19, 21 and 23) inches, and a series of mobile storage cabinets, including cupboards, and book trolleys. Some of these are fitted with display backs (chalkboard on one side, pin board on the other), and a range of trolleys has been designed to house the basic unit of storage, a plastics tray. Each child has one of these for his personal possessions, and the trays also store books, papers, pencils, scissors, etc.

It is, however, a sad reflection on the school furniture industry that the equipment had to be specially designed for a school like this. The teaching methods used there are by no means new, and for more than 15 years now teachers throughout the country have been struggling to apply these modern techniques in old, cramped buildings stocked for the most part with inflexible and inadequate furniture. Even the new schools have been pathetically furnished.

The reasons for this situation are complex, but the main difficulty has been the inability of most local authorities to get to grips with the problem – or even to recognise that one exists. The consortium approach which has enabled local authorities to achieve higher standards and greater flexibility in building design has only recently been applied to the design and development of school furniture, and the bulk of furniture used in schools today is chosen by local authority supplies officers who, often working to a very limited budget, buy 'loose' furniture (tables, chairs, desks, stools and some cupboards, etc) from a multitude of ranges offered by school furniture manufacturers. 'Fixed' furniture, on the other hand, is usually designed by local authority architects and the cost of these items is included in the building costs of any new school. Because of this artificial division between 'fixed' and 'loose' furniture, school furniture manufacturers and local authority designers had little incentive to design related ranges of storage and loose furniture, nor was much serious research into the general problem of storage in schools carried out.

Again, only a handful of authorities have had the resources and/or the initiative to establish their own design departments. The LCC[1] (now GLC), the largest authority in the country, has one; Kent County Council, another large authority, has had a furniture design department within its supplies division since the 'thirties, and Hertfordshire and Nottinghamshire have for many years now aimed at high standards. But these are isolated examples, and to obtain a clearer picture of the present methods of selecting school furniture, DESIGN sent questionnaires to over 150 local authorities in England to find out the way in which they select their school furniture.[?]

Although, regrettably, only 65 authorities have bothered to reply, their answers give a fair indication of the general approach to furniture design and selection. The questionnaire reveals that, among the smaller authorities, there is a furniture group working within the city architect's office in Manchester and Bristol Education Committee also employs a designer who, three years ago completely redesigned the furniture for the city's schools. Apart from these, 32 authorities have stated that they have some form of furniture selection committee, and in most cases this takes the form of ad hoc meetings between teachers, architects and supplies officers. The furniture is generally selected from manufacturers' catalogues, and 34 authorities stated they ask for modifications.

When authorities cannot find what they want, they submit their own specifications. In this case, furniture can be designed by teachers, architects and the supplies section. For example, in one instance "the staff of the education building surveyor" drew up

[1] London County Council
[?] Questionnaires were not sent to those authorities whose policies were already known. For example, Kent, Oxfordshire, Leicestershire and the ILEA were omitted, as they supplied information in interviews. Shropshire, West Sussex, Northants, Worcestershire, Derbyshire and Southend both were also omitted, as they are members of the Counties Furniture Group.

DESIGN 202

29

242 Pages from a recent issue of
Design magazine.

242

The very brief book list which follows these notes is not in any sense comprehensive. Each title would, however, offer something of value either to the teacher or the young person. For a much more complete coverage it is worth getting the *Library List* published by the Council of Industrial Design (price 1s 6d) which is a sectionalized list of books on all aspects of design.

There are three series of books which deserve special mention. First, Kurt Rowland's *Looking and Seeing* series published by Ginn and Company. These provide the basis of a complete visual education course and are supported by teacher's notes and filmstrips. In some respects the written material is too prescriptive, but the range of illustration is unique and every school would find it worth while to have a number of copies. Second, the series of paperbacks edited by John Lewis for Studio Vista. In this series David Pye's *The Nature of Design* is particularly good, but each title has its own specific merits. As the books are cheap, it might not be expecting too much if a school bought the whole set. Third, another series of paperbacks, called *Design Centre Publications*, which deal with particular aspects of domestic design (for example, there is one on *Bathrooms*, another on *Storage*). These are published by Macdonald & Co. in association with the CoID, and are cheap, short, and sensible.

Magazines are important. *Design,* published by the CoID and recently enlarged, is more or less essential, but *Ark,* published by the Royal College of Art, *Architectural Review,* and *Architectural Design,* and of course *Which?*, all have much to contribute. The colour supplements often discuss design but tend to do so in a superficial way – women's magazines, particularly *Woman* on interior design, are often better and more down to earth.

It is important not to stick to books or magazines solely about design or architecture. Weeklies like *New Society* and *The Economist* often discuss environmental problems, and the way these relate to economics or sociology. In another way, film, fashion, and pop music magazines obviously reflect on aspects of the studies discussed in this book. Looking still further afield, a book like the last volume of Trevelyan's *Illustrated English Social History* puts the origins of design into the perspective of the upheavals caused by the industrial revolution. Novels like Allan Sillitoe's *Loneliness of the Long Distance Runner*, or Saul Bellow's books about the United States, provide material for a good discussion of the cultural effects on individuals of the urban environment. Science fiction too has something to offer. A book like Isaac Asimov's *The Caves of Steel,* which looks to a future obsessed by the problem of getting men and robots to work together in harmony, is an exciting detective story that strikes at the roots of the dilemma facing men in a technological world. In the same way, *The Space Merchants,* by C. M. Kornbluth and Fredrik Pohl, is a highly relevant fable about a world where production equals morality, and society is run by giant advertising agencies.

SIR LEON BAGRIT. *The Age of Automation.* (Reith lectures, 1964). Weidenfeld & Nicolson (1965).

K. BAYNES. *Industrial Design and the Community.* Lund Humphries (1967).

H. DREYFUSS. *Measure of Man.* Whitney Library of Design (1959–60).

J. K. GALBRAITH. *The New Industrial State* (Reith lectures, 1966) in *The Listener* (17, 24 November, 1, 8, 15, 22 December 1966).

G. KEPES. *Language of Vision.* Paul Theobald (1949).

G. KEPES. *New Landscape in Art & Science.* Paul Theobald (1949).

G. E. KIDDER SMITH. *New Architecture of Europe.* Penguin Books (1962).

R. J. MITCHELL and M. D. R. LEYES. *A History of London Life.* Penguin Books (1963).

L. MUMFORD. *Art & Technics.* Oxford University Press (1952).

L. MUMFORD. *The City in History.* Pelican Books (1966).

I. NAIRN. *Nairn's London.* Penguin Books (1966).

G. NELSON. *Problems of Design.* Whitney Publications Inc. (1957).

N. PEVSNER. *High Victorian Design – a study of the exhibits of 1851.* Architectural Press (1951).

N. PEVSNER. *Pioneers of Modern Design.* Penguin Books (1960).

SIR GORDON RUSSELL. *Looking at Furniture.* Lund Humphries (1964).

T. WOLFE. *Kandy-kolored Tangerine Flake Streamline baby.* Cape (1966), paperback, Mayflower (1968)